THE GLOBAL INVESTOR RELATIONS REVOLUTION

KEY DRIVERS & FUTURE OPPORTUNITIES

A pioneering and critical assessment of the new dynamics in Investor Relations; where we are as an industry and profession, and the measures needed to further strengthen its reputation.

OSKAR YASAR

FEEDBACK ABOUT
THE GLOBAL INVESTOR RELATIONS REVOLUTION

"Tired of explaining what investor relations actually does? Hand them this book. The definitive resource on IR's strategic value." **Matthew Johnson, Group Communications Director, IR & CEO Office VODAFONE**

"Packed with insights from IR leaders across five continents. This is the global investor relations playbook you've been waiting for." **Laura Kiernan, Senior Vice President, RIVEL**

"The definitive roadmap for modern investor relations professionals. A must-read for anyone serious about elevating their IR career." **Matthew O'Keeffe, Managing Director, Global IR, FTI CONSULTING**

"The definitive strategic manifesto exploring the metamorphosis of Investor Relations from a mundane reporting function to a critical strategic intelligence hub that redefines corporate communication and market engagement." **Amani Korayeim, Director Corporate Product & Partnerships Europe/EMEA, EXTEL**

"Finally, a comprehensive global perspective on the IR profession's evolution. Essential reading for every IRO." **Anne Guimard, Founder & CEO, FINEO**

For my Papa

Published by Quartz Press

www.quartzpress.com

ISBN: 978-1-917329-69-9

BROOME
YASAR
PARTNERSHIP

Leading the global search for talent in investor relations & corporate affairs

IN ASSOCIATION WITH:

- The US Association of IR (NIRI), The UK IR Society, MEIRA (Middle East IR Association), DIRK (German IR Association), and additional contributions from the IR Associations of The Netherlands, Mexico, Canada, Switzerland, Italy, Spain, Turkey, Belgium, Israel, Hong Kong, South Africa, Romania and Australia
- IR Impact, *Formerly IR Magazine*
- Extel
- QuantiFire
- Storyline Communications

About the author: Oskar Yasar

O skar is regarded as the global leader in executive recruitment in investor relations and corporate affairs having been responsible for over 500 senior level appointments in numerous markets globally. He is the founding partner of the leading global executive recruitment firm, Broome Yasar Partnership, and also head of its US-based partner firm PLBsearch's IR practice.

London and New York based and with nearly 30 years' experience at the coal face of the industry, both on the IR advisory side and executive recruitment, Oskar has personally helped the careers of some of the world's leading IROs and corporate communications professionals.

Oskar is also a passionate advocate for the role of investor relations and corporate affairs and the future of the profession. As well as being the author of this book, *The Global IR Revolution*, he has also written two other studies, *From Investor Relations to Business Leadership - The pathway to CEO*, and *Key Building Blocks to Becoming a Standout IRO*, which showcases the significant transformation in the reputation of IR.

He is also co-author of the ground-breaking study, From *Band Leader to Master Conductor* on the transformation of the corporate affairs profession.

He is also the author of the soon-to-be published book, '**Stand Out or Stand Aside, the power of personal branding in the reputation industries.**'

For further information go to: *www.broomeyasar.com* or *www.broomeyasar.com/insights*

CONTENTS

INTRODUCTION

We are a global profession

We've come a long way. In investor relations today, we are more influential, more financially bolted and more rounded strategic communications professionals than at any point in our history. The best of us have not just boardroom access but are considered essential to the machinery of strategic decision making. Many are now transitioning into senior business leadership roles including CEOs and CFOs, and a number now sit on boards of listed companies as independent directors. This revolution is real and continues to be seen throughout the financial capital markets landscape. This book, we trust, will help to showcase just that.

But a key hurdle remains if we are to make that next step: interconnectedness. Most of us work in small teams, many as sole IROs. So our sense of being parts of a collective profession can easily become lost. Country IR associations bring us together locally but, at a global level, we still often lack a sense of ourselves as a recognized profession—an established, consistent international discipline, with shared goals and universal competencies.

I believe this is an obvious impediment to IR's professional growth. Sharing best practices, ideas, and solutions to common challenges is how every profession grows. On such matters hinge the next steps of IR's development. That's what *The Global IR Revolution* is all about.

After all, investors are global; markets are global; most of our organizations are global; and, increasingly, we ourselves are global entities in the international talent marketplace. *The Global IR Revolution* wraps its arms around the full sweep of investor relations across the world—where it has come from as a profession; how it has developed into a sophisticated executive function; its challenges and its abundant opportunities.

With the involvement of IR societies and associations on five continents, along with numerous high-profile IROs, association heads, advisors, and other senior business leaders, and responses from more than 1,000 interviews with leading global IROs, we believe this significant undertaking represents our industry's first ever "Global State of the Nation."

The aim is not just to create a landmark moment of stock-taking for investor relations, but to produce something you can use as a developmental tool to bring along the next generation. We want it to be a springboard for catapulting our profession into its best possible future.

OSKAR YASAR
Managing Partner
Broome Yasar Partnership

FOREWORD

By Laurie Havelock,

Editor, IR Impact (Formerly IR Magazine)

IR IS NOW A TRANSFORMED PROFESSION

Today, the importance of good shareholder communications is something recognized by CEOs, CFOs, investors, analysts and the wider financial world. That is a huge change. At *IR Impact*, in existence for some 35 years, we have been able to witness that transformation—the rapid rise of a profession, once sidelined, to becoming an accepted and global discipline. It's a transformation that we've reflected ourselves, evolving from being a printed magazine to a modern intelligence platform.

Today's capital markets are more complex by several degrees than those of the 1950s (when GE launched the first ever IR department), the 1960s (when the US's National Investor Relations Institute was established), or even the 1980s (when the UK's Investor Relations Society began life).

Alternative finance and a suite of new investment instruments have made the job of an IRO that much more difficult, with shareholders harder to identify and their expectations and preferences harder to discern. Now, shareholder communication is not as simple as keeping the markets informed: There are new goals, new topics of discussion and new audiences to win over. That all comes against a backdrop of increased regulatory scrutiny, the product of a rapidly-evolving marketplace and—regretfully—the lack of scruples shown by some participants.

It means the role of a modern-day IRO is pretty hard to sum up—and I say that after more than a decade of covering the industry for *IR Impact* (for so long, in fact, that we were published in print when I started!). One part is obvious: Any good IR practitioner has to be a complete expert in their company, aware of standardized metrics and personalized information alike, able to read a corporate story and understand the deepest accounting measures simultaneously.

It's also crucial to be able to communicate that in a variety of forums, whether in a formal gathering, a face-to-face meeting or—increasingly today—in a digital format. For that, it requires some of the most crucial bits of the human experience, the soft skills necessary to foster trusting relationships. The job requires juggling finance, communications, legal affairs, corporate strategy, governance and ESG knowledge all at once, and understanding of a global landscape that is increasingly fractured and differentiated. All of that, and you have to not treat any investors with preference over others. I can't imagine how you would organize and train yourself to do it all every day: I got a nosebleed just from writing it down.

And then there are the myriad ways that the role is morphing as we head into the latter part of the 21st century. Digital communications have changed how we all work and play, that's true, but for IROs it represents a quantum shift across their working lives. Whether it is dealing with an audience of retail investors who are clued up and ready to move markets, or keeping up with fresh social media trends (thankfully "IR via TikTok" hasn't yet taken off...), and the silent power of algorithmically-traded funds working through your shareholder register, the job will only get more complicated as the years roll by.

It's no wonder, then, that the strategic significance of the IR role is increasingly recognized by corporate decision makers, and why stories of IROs heading up to the C-Suite are becoming increasingly common. The findings of the *Global IR Revolution* show this, and also how far IR can still go. Congratulations to Oskar Yasar for showcasing the extraordinary transformation of an important profession.

1. OUR JOURNEY

Key Drivers

THE EARLY SHOOTS

S eventy years ago, a new role first began to emerge in a handful of American corporations, tasked with landing new retail investors. "Investor Relations Officers" (IROs) were somewhat lowly sales positions; pop-up roles to fulfil an immediate need during a boom in citizen speculation. Fast-forward to today and the executive status of many IROs bears testament to decades of change. But it also demonstrates a corporate profession that, unlike any other, has reinvented and reskilled and restaffed itself, over and over again, to adapt to the demands of each new era.

Many of the challenges we now face—a surge of unknown retail investors, hostile activism, dramatic regulatory changes and corporate governance scandals—are shockwaves IR has dealt with before.

Each time, chameleon-like, IR has refashioned itself. That is how it has survived. And that story of continual adaptation offers the best indication for how IR will likely thrive in response to the changes we face going forward.

THE "SALES ERA" OF IR

Our profession officially marks its foundation with the "shareholder communications" function at General Electric in 1953. But fledgling IR departments first really began springing up in large US companies during the late 1950s and early 1960s, all with the same goal: To land the new retail investors who had become, in a few short years, the biggest purchasers of US corporate stock.

The post-war boom had created wealth in small-town America and citizens were looking to invest it, exactly as ballooning US corporations were hunting investment for rapid expansion. It was a marriage made in heaven: By 1965, one in every six Americans was a company shareholder.

But it changed the dynamic between companies and investors. Corporations were accustomed to having a handful of incredibly wealthy individuals as shareholders—some old New England families; perhaps a pension fund or two—who were largely uninterested in hearing from the CEO or poring over the strategy, much less scrutinizing the day-to-day activities of the company. They kept their distance, read the Wall Street Journal, spoke to their own people and made their investment decisions from a distance. All they really expected were regular dividends.

Here now, though, in the American homeowner, was a large, diverse, millions-strong and very demanding group of private-citizen owners who expected accountability and communication about shareholdings that might represent their entire life savings. They wanted involvement for their investment.

Boardrooms were outraged. To be asked to answer to members of the general public on matters of strategy!

And so investor relations, having helped reel in those shareholders, was now tasked with managing their demands. IR went from being a brash sales and marketing function to an undisguised PR one, polishing up the company's image in service of a great story that would keep investors happy—and far from the CEO's door.

> There has been a dramatic increase in IR's workload, with more topics and more stakeholders to attend to. If you look 40-50 years ago, networking between IR professionals was crucial because the function was just beginning and there were not many people working in the field. Today it's key because IR is such a broad area, you need to count on all the expertise around you just to cope with all your duties.
>
> *Javier Rodriguez-Vega*
> Managing Director
> **SPANISH ASSOCIATION FOR IR (AERI)**

THE "PR ERA" OF IR

But it was a one-way conversation, usually mediated via the media, because these second-wave IR practitioners were almost always parachuted-in PR people (themselves in those days little more than smooth-talking, Madison Avenue press agents and publicists—and far from financially or strategically literate).

By the 1960s, annual reports had turned into huge, glossy sales brochures with little-to-no financial detail. Annual Meetings of Shareholders (or Annual General Meeting / AGM in the UK) were expensive sound-and-loud bonanzas in awe-inspiring locations but with little strategic substance. Gift baskets to shareholders became as common as anything resembling a financial report.

In a sense, this worked: Mom-and-pop investors weren't financially literate either, they just expected the right to be heard for their investments. But there was a problem: They also still wanted to meet the CEO and hear from the horse's mouth, not read about the company's decisions in some media puff-piece. CEOs continued to refuse, and investor relations professionals were simply not financially educated enough to give shareholders the detail they wanted.

An IRO today has to understand the numbers with the skill of an economist, craft it into a story with the skill of a communicator (and sell the equity story portion with the skill of a marketer), grasp the technology well enough to understand how it's changing stakeholder behavior, and understand the legal ramifications enough to know when lawyers are going to be required.

In German, we have a phrase *eierlegende wollmilchsau*—the "egg-laying, woolly, dairy pig"; an incredible, single animal that can provide you with eggs, milk, wool and meat! That's IR today.

Kay Bommer
Managing Director
GERMAN IR SOCIETY (DIRK)

THE FINANCIAL ANALYST ERA

The situation couldn't last. And when the model broke, it would leave IR in an existential crisis from which it only just emerged—by reinventing itself yet again, this time into a financial-analyst function.

First had come demand: The inexperienced post-war-boom shareholders had magically seen their investments turn into year-on-year gains for decades ... and they expected that to continue. But the stock market was not built to manage the vast numbers of new investors. By the early 1970s, a system built on volume was collapsing under the weight of it.

And when Wall Street crumpled, and so did company share prices—and those retail investors didn't get the unending growth they had come to expect—it precipitated change. Among the sweeping regulations that followed, those millions of retail investors were consolidated into a smaller group of relatively new financial entities: Institutional investors.

That made shareholders far more manageable for companies— tens of millions of people to answer to had become a few hundred—but it also fundamentally changed the conversation, and spelled trouble for IR. Companies were now accountable to entities representing huge, conjoined stock interests, staffed by highly economically literate Wall Street analysts. A gift basket wasn't going to cut it.

> Investor relations has undergone a huge transformation. Twenty years ago, it was treated almost as a back-office function and staffed, in a rather haphazard way, by a handful of lucky recruits making the jump from finance or communications. Today, IR is very much a front-of-house function; a valued profession in its own right.
>
> How did this transformation happen? Part luck, part judgment. It's clear that many talented individuals have chosen to join the industry over the last 20 years. But it has also benefitted from seismic regulatory changes. In the 1980s and '90s, it was arguably the equity analyst who occupied the pivotal role between the company and investor. All that changed in 2002 with Eliot Spitzer's move to separate equity research from investment banking. So began the slow death of equity research; MiFID II in 2018 was arguably just one more nail in the coffin.
>
> One consequence of the regulatory changes of the last 20 years has been to displace the analyst from a previously pre-eminent spot. Another has been to create a vacuum which the IRO has successfully filled.
>
> *Matthew O'Keeffe*
> **Managing Director**
> **FTI CONSULTING**

Plus, those analysts were already accustomed to dealing directly with the CFO, or the finance or treasury department. Now that they were representing vast institutional investments, that is what they continued to do.

The IR profession found itself cut out. There were diminishing numbers of retail investors, and institutional investors had no interest in IR's superficial positioning. The function had no clear purpose anymore; nobody to talk to.

Yet, CFOs still had a real need for investor relations—just of a different kind. Institutional investors had incredible power to make or break companies by shifting investments—or threatening to—and they soon began to flex that activist power. The late 1970s and 1980s became the zenith of the "corporate raider" era—activists who would often use borrowed funds to aggressively buy a large stake in a public company in order to exert control.

Since the CFO had limited bandwidth to handle this, and the CEO and the Board still refused to deal with investors (and had no desire to speak to statistically intimidating financial

---

I practiced IR in an era when we would send news by fax, when quarterly earning calls were considered an innovation, and when Selective Disclosure was a weird concept! So we have come a long way. Twenty-five years ago, we had to fight to be seen as anything more than "PR super experts," regurgitating press releases. Today, we are a recognized, respected and strategic profession, with a seat at the table.

Isabelle Adjahi
Vice President, Communications
CDPQ

---

analysts anyway), someone had to take on the responsibility of keeping institutional investors happy, raiders at bay, and the corporate ship steady.

Throughout the 1970s and '80s, therefore, investor relations was increasingly brought under the CFO and transformed from a pure publicity profession to a financial one. (The most glaring evidence of this was that it divorced itself from the PR industry publicly and acrimoniously by beginning its own professional associations, to remove any of the old taints of empty gloss.)

The function was revolutionized by sweeping rounds of new hiring—people with analyst or accounting skills to match those of the institutional investors. Mixed with the existing rump of market-literate communications professionals (mostly with financial PR backgrounds), the personnel profile of the function for the ensuing decades was set.

Over the last 20 years, the content of meetings with investors has undergone a major shift. IR used to be mostly about financial results—ensuring investors understood the reasons behind the numbers—and talking about "past" numbers (i.e., the previous quarter). Now, it has evolved well beyond "actual numbers" and well beyond the past into future expectations, industry movements and macro-specifics, competitors, economy and politics, ESG, and so on. It's a much broader conversation across a much longer timeline.

Başak Öge
Chair of Tüyid—The Turkish IR Association & Corporate Governance & Compliance Coordinator
TÜRKİYE ŞİŞE VE CAM FABRİKALARI A.Ş

This was now an analytical communications function focused on representing the company's financial value to investors. No more mass media, the role centered on one-on-one meetings with institutional shareholders and Wall Street brokers and analysts—and was now interpersonal, two-way communication.

THE FINANCIAL COMMUNICATIONS ERA

Not before time because, in the 1990s, the investor pressure only increased—for ever more disclosure; for cost and liability insight; for more detailed information on company performance; for voting rights on executive compensation; for insight into corporate strategy, "green" policy, governance, and much more.

Investor relations practitioners no longer had to be great at simply presenting a story. They now had to be equally good at defending the company's commercial strategy. When investors queried the company direction, acquisitions, reorganizations or product pipeline, it was IR who had to be able to answer.

Stakeholder research, audience mapping and positioning statements began to play a bigger part of the role, to head off potential queries in advance of calls. In short, IR became a proactive, disciplined communications role, getting ever closer to the profession we know today. (It also became global, as investor relations departments began springing up in European multinationals too.)

But while the focus and skillset had shifted, there was still one big developmental hurdle ahead: Balance. The communication with investors was not designed to reshape the company. The feedback gathered at investor events was rarely passed back up to the executive board. (They still didn't want to know what investors thought.)

Instead, although now financially literate, IR's communications role was still one heavily focused on persuasion—nakedly marketing the company's position to the buy and sell sides. Quite openly, IR's goal was to maximize the stock price. Good results were trumpeted to the heavens; bad results and poor investments were glossed over; sometimes even hidden.

THE ACTUARIAL ERA

That era came crashing to earth with the catastrophic corporate-accounting scandals of the early 2000s. IR would be forced to refocus all over again, and in dramatic ways.

Among the sweeping changes to the profession over the last 20 years, there has also obviously been a significant increase in the regulations imposed on issuers and therefore on IR functions. Much of this has fundamentally changed the day-to-day IR role, either directly, as with MiFID II, or indirectly, as with the many frameworks and standards around ESG, especially at a European level.

But that last example (ESG) is a great showcase for how IR has adapted to a new world with different requirements from new stakeholders, taking the lead on the issue (or, if not taking the lead, clearly really involved in it); and being willing to understand these issues and work on fostering them into a new buy-side/sell-side narrative.

Javier Rodriguez-Vega
Managing Director
SPANISH ASSOCIATION FOR IR (AERI)

For not only did corporates come under the microscope in the aftermath, so too did investor relations—especially following Enron's collapse and the revelations that it (along with Tyco and others) had been brazenly miscommunicating their true valuation for years.

The tsunami of shareholder communications regulations that followed were a wake-up call for the profession. What resulted, after some soul searching, was a strengthening of IR's operating procedures—but also, ironically, growth in its power and influence.

For there were now waves of new requirements to meet around corporate governance and accuracy in public disclosure. Sarbanes-Oxley (2002) alone demanded an eye-watering list— real-time disclosures; off-balance-sheet transaction disclosures; pro forma financial disclosures; management assessment of internal controls; corporate responsibility for financial reports; and much more.

That meant it was now a hard legal necessity for companies to have informed and comprehensive communication with shareholders—on a greater scale, and with greater attention-to-detail than ever before. Having sound, reliable, accountable and well-informed IR was now a basic necessity.

It also made IR a very visible company asset—no longer just acting as a convenient buffer between investors and the ExCo, but now as a buffer between the company and legal and financial ruin.

From Sarbanes-Oxley to the present day, IR became, in many ways, an actuarial function, as much protecting the company from risk as increasing its share value. Little wonder that, throughout this period, more and more professionals with legal, governmental, regulatory and public-affairs backgrounds began joining IR, adding to the diverse cocktail of financial PR practitioners, analysts, accountants and finance graduates already making up this most complex and diverse of professions.

Today vs. a decade ago? Teams are bigger. Finance knowledge is a must. And no IRO I know would report to anyone other than the CEO or CFO today.

Karen Keyes
Head of Investor Relations
CANADIAN TIRE CORPORATION

The metamorphosis away from a purely balance-sheet-driven function has happened. At senior level in large caps, IROs have become representatives of the institution. They not only 'sell' the equity and bond story, but they bring together all stakeholders to help them understand what the company is really about from a strategic point of view.

Today, that clearly means, in part, bringing ESG and sustainability into their discussions. Indeed, investors today demand far deeper underlying knowledge from IROs on ESG and the long-term sustainability strategy than they did 20 years ago, especially in the context of climate change. These are considered such fundamental issues today that we see both equity and debt investors asking a lot of questions of IROs—and expecting them to be not just supremely well-informed but able to define the company's mitigating actions to risks.

Piero Munari
Co-Founder - Arwin&Partners
& Former Chair
ITALIAN INVESTOR RELATIONS SOCIETY

THE INTANGIBLES ERA

And so, in many ways, IR has remained to the present day—just increasingly so. The 2008 financial crisis brought further regulations, and the West's economic stagnation since 2008, and the decline in stock market listings, have only increased the demand for a persuasive conduit to investment capital.

But over the last decade, to this heady brew has increasingly been added one more revolutionary element, finally drawing a hard line under the "number-crunching" IR function of old, driving us towards the nuanced, multi-skilled communications profession we know today: Corporate purpose.

The focus of investor reporting today has increasingly become not just compliance with formal regulatory requirements, but also metrics for intangible assets such as brand equity, intellectual capital, corporate purpose, and, most recently, ESG and sustainability, with large forfeits for non-compliance. From its "communications" era to its "financial" era, investor relations has increasingly moved into its "intangibles" era.

> There have been significant changes in IR over the last 10-20 years. I have been in the profession since 2000 and, besides having truly enjoyed it, have personally witnessed significant elevation in the role (and compensation) at public companies throughout the 2000s.
>
> *Laura Kiernan*
> **Senior Vice President**
> **RIVEL, INC**

WHERE ARE WE NOW?

This perfect storm of factors has created all of the growth in the profession outlined throughout this book—heightened reputation; executive reach; ballooning remit; growing teams; the convergence with corporate communications and the twin status of being a trusted "outside-in" consigliere to the ExCo and a reliable executive proxy in front of major investors. The profession has truly come of age.

The evidence is there in its hiring profile. With the increasing complexity and importance of the role, a new generation of IRO is now being brought in by major businesses: Armed with executive backgrounds, business acumen, M&A experience, MBAs and wide-ranging operational expertise, these are no longer the finance or communications juniors of old. These are serious boardroom players. IR is now seen by the senior talent market as a solid springboard onto the executive

---

The changes to the profession in the past five to ten years have been material. IR today needs a far broader and more in-depth knowledge of the company—both debt markets, insurance markets and investor organizations around non-financial developments.

Increased virtual meetings have also increased the number of touchpoints throughout the year with investors. And, in very recent years, the world has seen a lot of significant changes and surprises (Covid, war in Ukraine, Russia sanctions, cost of living crises, rapid inflation) that companies need to respond to—all further adding to the demand on, and expectations of, IR, underlining this greater complexity.

Andreas Bork
Vice-President, IR & ESG
SHELL
& Former Chair of NEVIR, The Dutch IR Association

---

team—because it's seen by the ExCo as the sharp end of the reputational spear.

But that elevation in stature and broadening of remit has also created obvious anomalies—and created uncertainty about the future that lies ahead.

First, while in large-cap companies and with the best IROs, investor relations has become an indispensable boardroom advisor, the decline in company listings (and challenges for small- and medium-cap companies to list) is threatening to hollow out the profession elsewhere. Overall, it seems likely that there will be fewer IR departments because fewer companies will be seeking public investment.

Second, ESG and sustainability have become absolutely intrinsic to the role because understanding the parameters of purpose-led investment has become so important to ensuring a stable and fair valuation, as well as to securing new capital. Yet it is so important to corporates that most are now increasingly

---

The progression of IR reflects the importance of approaching our profession with a spirit of craftmanship. The best IROs are always hungry, asking questions and deepening their knowledge and understanding. Developing partnerships internally and externally is critical, as our roles often bridge the gap between the street and "the company"—IR has become a teacher, and that impacts our specific companies, our personal reputations and our industry. That role we have as storytellers has an opportunity to create value daily, which I find fascinating.

Kevin Kim
VP Investor Relations
SYSCO

constructing permanent departments dedicated to the issue. Has IR staked too much of its internal value on its ownership of the sustainability narrative?

Third, the profession may be heading for an all-out turf war with corporate affairs—and this time, it won't just lead to a lot of hot air about the "need for greater alignment."

For the complex, interlaced factors that have driven the growth of IR's power and influence over the last decade have driven a comparable growth in influence and size for other communications functions. They, too, have been responding to the maelstrom of modernity—to volatile public activism in a purpose-driven, social-media-enabled, channel-independent world. They too have professionalized, developed and grown. They too increasingly have executive access—or an actual boardroom seat—because they have come to the same conclusions as IR about their value point: Managing the company narrative holistically across all audiences.

IR is more than just delivering accurate and timely information to the investment community—it is a strategic asset that enhances a company's brand and credibility. Companies that effectively leverage their IR capabilities through a well-defined strategy and excellent execution can create sustainable value for their business and stakeholders alike.

Aslı Selçuk,
Founder & CEO
ASLI SELÇUK ADVISORY
Former Chairperson
TURKISH IR SOCIETY (TUYID)

The remits of IROs and heads of corporate affairs have become virtually indistinguishable as a result: Reputational guardianship, sustainability, brand equity, human capital, ESG. Any serious head of corporate affairs today sees themselves as the natural, executive-level air-traffic-control function for the company's integrated public positioning—and is absorbing more and more adjacent functions (such as brand, marketing, strategy and ESG) into their remit to achieve it. In a world where the boundaries between consumers, employees, media and market actors are increasingly hard to define, where does that leave an independent IR function?

So, we arrive at today's crossroads: Investor relations is more sophisticated, more complex and more in demand than ever before. Its leading exponents have made themselves essential leaders. A rising tide of issues in the business environment ever-increasingly make IR indispensable.

Yet challenges lie ahead, and some are truly existential—the still-unknowns of AI; the decline in publicly listed companies; the internal landgrabs around brand narrative, reputation and purpose. But our history gives us hope. We have the strength of knowing, from 75 years' evidence, that ours is a profession built on relentless adaptability; on seizing opportunities; on consistently developing the best skills to deliver value to meet the challenges of that era.

There was a former CFO of Siemens who was asked "What is IR?" and he said, "Clearly it's a financial function. It's clearly about the money and the numbers, so it needs to sit with me." And it then came to the CEO, who said, "No, no, it's so strategic, so important, it needs to sit with me because, as the CEO, I need to know how the capital markets think." And so he ended up taking the IRO as his direct report.

That CEO got it. He understood the value point in IR today.

Kay Bommer
Managing Director
GERMAN IR SOCIETY (DIRK)

2. OUR PRESENT

The profession's new normal

A TRANSFORMED MARKETPLACE

M arkets never sit still. So, for a function whose *raison d'être* is to be touch-responsive to investors' shifting moods, the transformation in investor relations in recent years can inevitably be traced to equivalent seismic activity in the financial landscape, completely changing the ecosystem in which today's IR professional has to operate.

From restrictive regulation to bursting bubbles, from commercial globalization to investor atomization, from ESG to AI, any analysis of where investor relations is currently positioned—and why—must begin with an understanding of the continued disruptions in the ecosystem it has been serving.

Our interviewees highlighted many issues from recent years—or looming in our near future—that have fundamentally changed today's IRO role.

Major disruptions have become very frequent, be it MiFID II, Covid-19, algo-trading trends, military wars and so on—right down to the emergence of topics like ESG in discussions with investors. IROs have been forced to be very agile in terms of dealing with these "swans" of all colors proactively. It's meant they have to be extremely well-connected to world events and crises, and to adapt their way of doing business quickly, with a sense of urgency, to remain in the game.

Başak Öge
Chair of Tüyid—The Turkish IR Association & Corporate Governance &
Compliance Coordinator
TÜRKİYE ŞİŞE VE CAM FABRİKALARI A.Ş

Market turmoil, pandemics, wars and shifts in the financial markets have all impacted the IRO and the way the function both integrates internally and communicates externally with the market. The complexity of the market has diversified—in addition to the well-known listed exchanges have come dark pools available to all stakeholders. MiFID II (Markets in Financial Instruments Directive II—a European regulatory framework) has encouraged more direct and more frequent engagement between companies and their shareholders. The demands of corporate governance have put our organizations under an intense spotlight.

All this and successive waves of sustainability demands from consumers and investors has generated a whole new universe of work—information, requirements and strategic know-how that any serious player in the profession now has to be fully across. Meanwhile, the shift of assets to hedge strategies and into passive funds, as well as the rise of activist and ESG-led investors, have increased the importance of having a high-performing IR function capable of making smart business decisions in the service of the company's reputation.

No one factor could be said to be the catalyst forcing a rethink of IR's remit. Uncertainty is a constant in the capital markets, but so is the complexity of the inter-dependent variables

---

Investor Relations has changed from a reactive role to a proactive one, whereby we now develop IR strategies to avoid issues rather than react to issues.

Nathalie Megann
President and Chief Executive Officer
CANADIAN IR INSTITUTE (CIRI)

driving that disruption. And since volatility in world markets is now the "new normal," it means that IR has had to become better at managing uncertainty, framing guidance to executive teams and investors in terms of a range of possible outcomes rather than the confident absolutes in which it perhaps once trafficked.

More than anything else, therefore, the key to IR's development has been the agility and adaptability that has been its calling card over the last 70 years.

The day-to-day IR role is dramatically different today. Digital platforms have become essential tools for communicating with investors, and have enabled companies to reach a much larger audience. The function now involves more analysis of ESG factors and focuses on developing relationships with a broader range of investors. IR professionals are increasingly involved in corporate decision-making, even contributing to overall strategy, and are recognized as an essential strategic function in helping management better understand the market and communicate more effectively with investors. As a result, relationships with other colleagues, including those in marketing and communications, have improved too. It's a different ballgame.

Maximilian Zimmermann Canovas
President and Cofounder of INARI and Investor Relations and Sustainability Director at Grupo Hotelero Santa Fe

---

A LEADERSHIP REPUTATION

Seventy years ago, investor relations was a buffer—a function specifically designed to keep shareholders from the boardroom door. Far from being invited in to provide strategic insight, the IRO's unambiguous job description was to stay well away. How times have changed.

Today, external changes (notably regulation and the rise of purpose-led investing) and internal ones (particularly IR's professionalization) have meant that the most successful IROs are more influential and respected strategic communications professionals than ever before—and the best are not just "in the room" for key decisions, their input is being actively sought in advance to inform those judgements.

One of the biggest catalysts has been the external transparency pressure put on management. From Sarbanes-Oxley to MiFID to the recent spate of ESG-related reporting obligations like SFDR, CEOs can no longer get away with using investor relations as a firewall—because they themselves have to answer to the markets and their regulatory demands.

It has created a proximity between IROs and senior executives unprecedented in the profession's history. With that has come a much deeper boardroom understanding of what IR does—and what great IR can do—and a newfound respect for its unique insights and capabilities.

There have been some major shifts in the regulatory environment and in the banking industry that have placed more responsibility on companies to manage and market their own stories. Additionally, IROs have had to speak on behalf of CEOs and CFOs, requiring them to have in-depth communications about not only income statements, balance sheets and cash flow statements but also corporate strategy, capital allocation and relative valuation.

Laura Kiernan
Senior Vice President
RIVEL, INC

The result? Many IR professionals today are playing a much more substantial role than they were in the past—well beyond the traditional remit of fostering dialogue with the financial community about the company story and its quarterly performance, or being perceived as a support function that simply requests information to satisfy the requirements of the financial markets.

My experience is that IROs have a seat at the table, and it is not uncommon to see them regularly participating in C-level, executive committee, audit committee, disclosure committee and Board-level discussions. Compensation for IROs has increased over the years commensurate with that level of experience and expertise. So we currently stand at a point where IROs are more highly valued than any time in the past—both internally by the management and Board, and externally by investors, analysts, bankers, and financial media. The skillset is rare, and hence qualified IROs remain in strong demand.

Laura Kiernan
Senior Vice President
RIVEL, INC

The reputation of IR as an industry has definitely changed over the last 20 years. Where the CEO and CFO might previously have seen the IRO as a bag-carrier, they now very often view the IRO as an ambassador for the whole company to the investment community. And this is about function as well as perception: the IRO is often now deployed by the management team as the first line of defense against any incoming investor interest. So the IRO becomes a hugely important filter; it is up to her or him to assess interested investors and to determine whether they are worthy of a further meeting.

Matthew O'Keeffe
Managing Director
FTI CONSULTING

Instead, today IR has come to be seen as a business partner not only protecting the company's reputation in the markets, but bringing added value internally—by bringing external insights into the business to support strategy development and, more recently in many businesses, going further than that to become a catalyst for change in a wide range of business areas, even formulating decisions about company strategy and corporate governance.

These are fundamental changes and they all stem from the same source: An increasing recognition among CEOs and Boards of Directors that IR can be both influential on investors as well as a great first-hand source on the public viewpoint—that it sits in a unique position to be a genuine, free-flowing two-way communication channel between the C-Suite and those financing the company, and that it has the complex diversity of business, financial and communications skills to meet that need.

> Our insights are requested by the CEO and Board as key inputs to strategic decision-making (market feedback, investors' financial expectations, etc.). The Board and management team rely on us more and more—it's difficult for them to make a strategic decision without having consulted us. These are big changes. Our input is also requested by other colleagues, as we can provide sector information, peer data, market perception and so on for internal projects. But all of that has also raised the expectations bar for IR: Internally, we need to be able to operate at management level.
>
> *Juan Gaitan*
> **Director of Investor Relations**
> **CELLNEX TELECOM**

ENHANCED STATUS WITH INVESTORS

Long silences—and empty halls—once greeted the IRO who informed shareholders that a meeting would be "IR only." Although that ceiling has not quite been smashed through, our interviewees felt that a corner had certainly been turned in recent years. Investors today increasingly recognize that IR no longer represents a thinly disguised marketing push, or an emissary sent out to deflect them with superficial answers. It is an informed function with broad company knowledge, and the boardroom access to be seen as a reliable proxy for the CEO.

"When I started ten years ago, there was almost a reluctance among investors to engage directly with IR and a feeling that 'IR only' meetings were insufficient," says Matthew Johnson, Group Communications Director, IR & CEO Office at Vodafone. "But given the vast improvements in the profession since then, that has changed significantly: IR is now not just accepted, but expected to be as on top of every issue as the CEO or CFO would be."

If nothing else, the sheer breadth of company knowledge an IRO now must hold to execute the role—and the complexity and nuance of the position today—has changed the dynamic. It has made the best IROs extremely well informed, which has made them a provably reliable source of information. It has even increased investor belief that—often—clearer, truer and more comprehensive answers to questions can be sourced from an IRO than from members of the senior executive team.

> Without a doubt, external expectations and impressions of IR have grown. Investors now expect to have the same dialogue—often even more nuanced and tailored dialogue—with IR as they would with the CEO and CFO. They understand that the CEO and CFO are not always available and so count on IROs to handle their discussions.
>
> *Philip Ludwig*
> Vice-Chair
> BELGIAN IR ASSOCIATION &
> Investor Relations Director
> MELEXIS

MIFID II: THE GREAT CAPABILITY SHIFT

MiFID II (2018) has not been the first regulation to alter the relationship between firms and the financial community over the last 70 years. But for public companies in the UK and EU (and indeed for any multinational, given MiFID II's significant extraterritorial reach), it has been the most profound recent

> The most significant external development in recent years has been the changing role of the sell-side. After regulatory changes in Europe, the volume of direct communication between the investment community and companies has increased exponentially. That has required IR to invest more time and energy in understanding who their shareholders and targets actually are, and to 'own' the corporate-access function that was previously effectively outsourced to the sell-side.
>
> *Matthew Johnson*
> Group Communications Director,
> IR & CEO Office,
> VODAFONE

change, catalyzing an increase in direct contact with investors, an overhaul of IR's skills requirements—and a bigger workload.

IR professionals now need to maintain more comprehensive records of their interactions with investors; have more coordination with legal departments to ensure compliance; and even adapt their approach to investor events, after MiFID II altered how asset managers pay for corporate access.

It has also meant ever harder work on investor segmentation: Due to MiFID II's focus on investor protection and unbundling of research costs from execution, IR professionals now need to work more closely with finance and legal departments to segment their investor base effectively, understanding different needs and providing tailored services accordingly.

MiFID II absolutely changed the way companies engage with stakeholders. First, investors now have a direct line to IR teams, as do IROs introducing themselves to an investor. And with the ongoing consolidation on the buy-side, and as the hedge fund landscape continues to change as firms close and new ones open, a good CRM tool is critical for IROs to keep track.

Second, if direct engagement increased significantly post-MIFID II, then during Covid it just ballooned. And now that large buy-side firms have in-house experts to manage the engagement process, they're no longer using brokers to facilitate that. So, as that trend for brokers 'doing it all' has changed over the years, the IRO must now take some of the responsibility directly for engagement.

Lorna Davie
President
IR CLUB SWITZERLAND
& Former Director, Investor Relations
CREDIT SUISSE/UBS

All of this in addition to the biggest fallout: A precipitous decline in sell-side analysis. One study suggested that, for the average EU firm in the first year of MiFID II's implementation alone, there was a 10% decline in analyst following.[1] Research from 2023 suggests that the sell-side analyst industry has now fallen off a cliff: Between 2011 and 2021, firm-specific coverage globally declined 17.8%. In the EU, it was 28.5%[2]. IROs have certainly noticed (see QuantiFire research).

It has pushed IR to develop new analytical skills, but also meant that IROs now typically have to field more direct requests: Investors now rely more on their own in-house research, which in turn has led to more frequent information requests and discussions with IROs.

So it now falls to IROs much more than ever before to feed investors with more analytical tools, and to be more involved one-to-one, scrutinizing investors' valuation models to ensure fair value. On the plus side, this has all opened up channels of communication, trust and responsiveness— cementing, in some cases, the relationship between IROs and the investment community. On the minus side, it is another way in which the workload and pressure on IR have increased beyond measure.

---

[1] Lang, Mark, Jedson Pinto, and Edward Sul. "MiFID II unbundling and sell-side analyst research." Journal of Accounting and Economics (2023): 101617.
[2] Hettler, Barry, Justyna Skomra, and Arno Forst. "The great sell-side sell-off: evidence of declining financial analyst coverage." Accounting Research Journal 36.2/3 (2023): 290-305.

Heads of IR: Investor Feedback is Failing…and getting worse

IRO Satisfaction with Support from the Sell Side: Past 10 Years*

	Very Poor (-2)	Poor (-1)	Neutral (0)	Good (1)	Very Good (2)
Responsiveness				0.84 / 0.80	
Quality of IR Support				0.75 / 0.71	
Quality of Meetings				0.69 / 0.54	
Quality of Research				0.66 / 0.54	
Accuracy of Forecasts				0.57 / 0.54	
Quality of Feedback		-0.02	0.06		

Typical Comments:

"It's clear that the sell side are overstretched having suffered a death from a thousand cuts"

"We have seen that the banks corporate access teams are downgraded/overloaded in terms of demands on their staff"

"Sell side juniorization and hollowing out has accelerated"

Pre-MiFID II (5 Yrs: 2013 - 2017)
Post-MiFID II (5 Yrs: 2018 - 2022)

*QuantiFire has run an annual membership survey for the IR Society since 2013. Data is filtered to only show results based on 425 responses from Heads of IR.

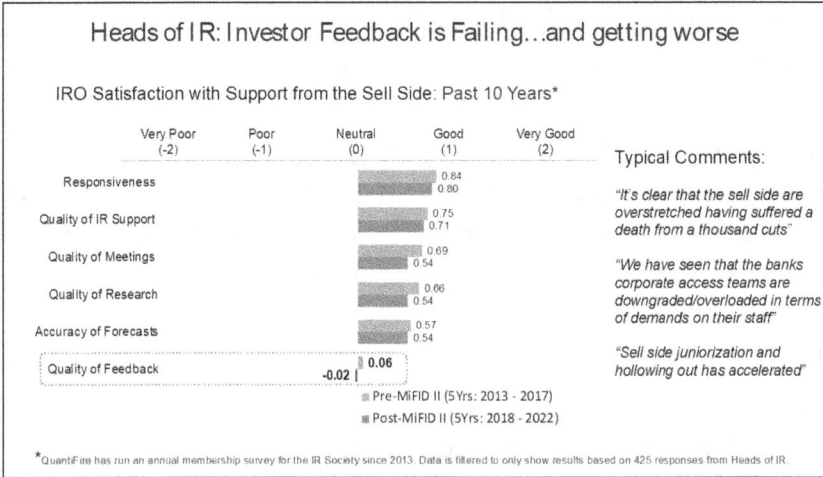

Analysis by QuantiFire, investigating ten years' annual surveys of UK Heads of IR on the quality of sell-side analysis, shows a clear decline in satisfaction pre- and post-MiFID II

"MORE THAN THE NUMBERS": THE RISE OF ESG AND PURPOSE

But MiFID II increased the demand for high-level financial, analytical and research skills in IR right at the moment the function was expanding its competencies and worldview well beyond the balance sheet.

For, of all the external changes to the profession over the last decade, perhaps none has had more transformational impact than the rise of purpose-led investing, which has especially grown in significance and interest among active investment managers. According to the Edelman Trust Barometer from 2020, a staggering 84% of institutional investors said that "maximizing shareholder returns was no longer the primary goal of the corporation"; that "business leaders must commit to balancing the needs of shareholders with those of employees, customers, suppliers and local communities."

It has meant that today's IRO has to be vastly more conversant with a broad range of issues, from its social improvement strategy to its operations globally, to be able to articulate the company's purpose just as well as its pricing.

It also means that the company needs to be able to report in fundamentally different ways—both its metrics, and its reporting media. In some cases, that is still very much an evolving space. But as this book goes to print we have seen the rise of Trumpism in business with significant possible repercussions on how businesses prepare their messaging for sustainability and ESG questions—so even after the past few years of companies transforming their policies to fit a new agenda, will we see the tables turning 180 degrees?

But we know that companies still need to formulate their programmes within the current ESG backdrop, so if anything drastic happens, it's business as usual.

Around purpose, IROs now have to measure, analyze and report additional information that does not yet have a universally defined global framework, for example. For financial measures, US companies have been using GAAP or IFRS to report for decades (and, with their increasing convergence, that reporting framework has become ever-more universal globally). With ESG, though, the frameworks are still coming together, so the way things are measured differs between companies.

But above all, it has changed the way IR has to approach the entire job. The modern IR person is expected to know as much about their organization's energy consumption, supply chain, Board composition, remuneration policy, team formation and engagement as they do about the last quarter of financial performance. That is a fundamental change from the "bean counter" and "financial reporter" stereotype of even just a few years ago.

ESG and sustainability engagement is critical, with increasing disclosure requirements and ESG communications very much integrated into the day-to-day role of an IRO. Companies also need to understand how investors incorporate sustainability into their investment decision-making process, and investors must work collaboratively with companies to understand how sustainability issues are being addressed. Global standards and frameworks are also creating a level playing field for disclosure globally.

Laura Hayter
CEO
THE IR SOCIETY, UK

A TRANSFORMED CLIENT BASE

In IR's early days, the company's shareholder register might fit on a single sheet of paper. The investment strategy of that small group of high-net-worth individuals mostly amounted to buy-and-hold, long-term accumulation of shares in fundamentally sound companies; dividend yield was the main determinant of their investment choices; and the transfer of paper-based share certificates took an age, deterring all but established players.

A much broader shareholder landscape has existed for some time, of course. But during the 2010s, IR's client base has become vastly more complex all over again: A surge of self-taught, socially-conscious, young, tech-savvy or short-termist investors; retail investors fed by real-time analysis and fast digital trading capabilities; or algo-traders, immune to persuasively worded reports and absent from investor meetings.

What changed? The democratization of investing with the accessibility of online trading platforms, commission-free trading, and social media all contributed to increased participation by retail investors in the late 2000s.

> There is a younger generation of investors who are instinctively more purpose-driven in how they invest. On top of that, within your institutional investors, you increasingly have two different sets of stakeholders—fund managers who take the investment decision, and then the governance, sustainability or ESG team, who are concerned with protecting their investors' reputations. And in some companies they work closely together, and in other companies they're sworn enemies. But you need to deal with both. So it's another complexity ESG has added—it has doubled your audience within institutional investors, at least in sectors with high ESG risk like energy, mining, heavy industry.
>
> *Andreas Bork*
> Vice-President, IR & ESG
> SHELL

> AI can now scan a company or sector in minutes, or scrape video and written content from a number of sources to corroborate the language and mood of the company's equity story. So functions like communications, marketing, stakeholder management, PR, sustainability, CSR and ESG are no longer separate and siloed from investor relations. The markets that IROs serve can—and do—obtain information from multiple sources, and IROs need to understand the messaging being put out through all public platforms.
>
> *Debbie Millar*
> Chair
> IR SOCIETY OF SOUTH AFRICA

That trend has only accelerated in recent years: Many active investors today are millennials and Generation Z—more tech-savvy, preferring digital platforms and mobile apps—with the rise of fintech in particular inspiring them to engage in capital markets. That is a far cry from the investor base at the beginnings of the IR profession in the post-war era (which mostly consisted of a handful of "old money" families and large institutions), or even the heavy-hitting City & Wall Street firms of a decade ago.

Meanwhile, algorithmic trading strategies and data-driven approaches have become a hallmark of institutional investment, coinciding with a shift from active investment towards passive. And all this while tech entrepreneurs are participating in private markets, injecting venture capital and angel investing to destabilize the standard models. And on top of that, the globalization of capital markets has led to an increase in cross-border investors, with sovereign wealth funds, pension funds, and other institutional investors from different regions actively participating in international markets.

Since the millennium, the IR audience demographics have shifted profoundly in terms of both the types of funds we interact with and the profile of individual investors. Historically, the IR audience was more focused on owners of the company. The shift in assets from traditional, long-only active institutions to rules-based funds and short-term-horizons investment has had a profound impact on what we need to know for those investors and how we need to interact with them about it. Meanwhile, the profile shift has been from Gen-X, male WASPs to a younger, more diverse universe. That changes the nature of how we communicate.

Matthew Johnson
Group Communications Director,
IR & CEO Office,
VODAFONE

"The rise of the retail investor has been a clear trend in the UK and especially the US, spurred on by the COVID period when sheer boredom led a whole new generation of investors into the stock market," says Matthew O'Keeffe of FTI Consulting. "In my opinion, no company has adequately solved the problem of how to engage with such a disparate audience. The solution may well be found in better use of digital channels. Meanwhile, the rise of new regions as sources of potential capital has led the intrepid IRO on ever more interesting journeys. The traditional road trips to the UK, the US and continental Europe are no longer sufficient for a company looking to cover all bases. The rise of sovereign wealth funds in the Middle East is the highest profile example of a region, abundant in capital, that has appeared on the map in recent years."

The last 20 years has really coincided with the shift of assets to hedge strategies and passive funds, as well as the rise of activist, governance and ESG-led investors.

Changes in the information landscape have also changed the role. Many painful discussions about xbrl later, we have ultimately arrived at the same goal via better search technology that removes the onus on IR and finance! With everything we do at Canadian Tire Corporation now online and searchable, investors have access to a richness of data—financial, strategic, and in multiple media— as well as the ability to screen firms in minutes. It's something I could never have imagined when I first started in IR.

That availability of data, with faster processing, has led a meaningful shift towards passive investing and algorithmic trading that was still in its early stages when I first joined. All of that means more precision about which types of investors you are targeting and the different techniques required to communicate with each of them.

Karen Keyes
Head of Investor Relations
CANADIAN TIRE CORPORATION

Connecting and communicating with—and understanding the needs of—this mushrooming group of infinite complexity has presented a generational challenge for IROs.

TECHNOLOGY: THE CHANGED MECHANICS

Communication growth and technological advancement go hand in hand. Little wonder that IR has been radically altered many times by explosions in global communication technology from 1980s' faxing, to the 1990s' email and internet, to the 2000s' social media and smartphone apps.

Today, those technologies, and the complexities they brought to the role, look quaint. Digital tools and platforms are now intimately integrated into standard investor outreach in ever more complex combinations, and advanced analytics are transforming IR's ability to leverage strategic opportunities.

All multinationals today maintain sophisticated online investor portals with up-to-date information, financial reports and presentations. Virtual meetings are now standard for earnings calls and investor presentations. Twitter (now X), LinkedIn, and other social media allow real-time, interactive engagement. Automation tools efficiently generate and disseminate earnings reports.

But it has been the leveraging of technology for the internal elements of the role that have most profoundly shaped its strategic capability. Today, CRM systems help track individual investor preferences and streamline communications. Analytics synthesize investor behavior and sentiment with market trends, and are often integrated with financial reporting systems, allowing for a seamless analysis of a range of financial and investor performance metrics and KPIs. Overall, big data has allowed IR professionals to analyze vast volumes of market data, investor feedback, global trends, sentiment and financial metrics to make informed predictions about future investor behavior.

And now the profession faces an AI-turbo-charged future, threatening probably the biggest overhaul of the role in its history. Few of us can realistically conceptualize how much more technologically advanced the role will get—or how near on the horizon that transformation will be—but it is not hard to imagine a day when much of the work around reporting the quarter, and some of the work around investor targeting, could be automated and driven by AI—potentially releasing IR into a more strategic role, evaluating and shaping the company's positioning.

> My perception is that, because the IR function has a unique, end-to-end overview of the company, the IR community increasingly consist of non-finance specialists like engineers, lawyers or doctors depending on the sector the company is operating in. Because that is the expectation from investors beyond the financials—that you are a true subject-matter expert in your sector, in your commercial market, and in your products and services, so that you can report on the company's non-financial plans and performance as ably as you can talk about the P&L.
>
> *Andreas Bork*
> Vice-President, IR & ESG
> SHELL

A DIFFERENT CONVERSATION

Those changes in both the investor base and investor strategy have meant that today's shareholder conversation is materially different from that of the past.

The rise of ETFs and indexing have made some shareholder "communication" a matter of standardizing reporting metrics to ensure the company's inclusion on indices according to their screening methodologies. For the surge of retail investors, it has meant better audience mapping and channel segmentation. And for the classic face-to-face interactions with major shareholders, it has meant a more diverse conversation about a far broader range of issues.

For those institutional investors today, the numbers matter less than they ever have. Where once IR was mostly about ensuring investors understood the story behind the financial results—what they meant, the decisions that had led to them, and what was being done about them. The modern fund manager, in contrast, expects a complex, all-encompassing and *operational* discussion with IR about every aspect of the company's affairs—from its overall global investment strategy to the intricate detail of its day-to-day operations.

And where once that conversation was about the previous financial quarter, today it is as likely to be about expectations for the future—industry movements, buyer mood, economic forecasts, what the changing political weather will mean, how

> Investors today don't just expect IROs to be responsive, accessible, and clear in our communications. They're demanding we be a "jack of all trades"—able to talk about modelling, strategy, operations, and so on. It's a different conversation. They also expect more access (by leveraging virtual meetings) and, since COVID, they're more comfortable reaching out at any time.
>
> *Ashish Kohli*
> VP Investor Relations
> GENERAL MOTORS

supply chains are likely to be affected, and much more. "It's a much broader conversation across a much longer timeline," as one of our interviewees said.

And how that is communicated? That has changed beyond measure too, with a wealth of virtual and electronic communications channels now a standard part of the IRO's

In the vast majority of the 1,500+ interactions I have with investors each year, it is rare for me to spend much time discussing financial data. For some time, good IR has extended well beyond numbers into deep understanding of corporate and market structure, and commercial and operational performance.

The next phase, I think, is to fully integrate our ESG understanding: The modern IR person should be expected to know as much about their organization's energy consumption, supply chain, Board composition, remuneration policy, team formation and engagement as they do about the last quarter financial performance.

Matthew Johnson
Group Communications Director,
IR & CEO Office,
VODAFONE

As in many fields, technology has been a powerful catalyst for change in IR. The use of advanced analytical tools, AI, and machine learning in IR has not only enhanced the efficiency of operations but has also improved the accuracy of forecasts and risk assessments. The digitization of the disclosure control and ethics process has further streamlined operations, enabling brands to maintain transparency and build trust with investors.

Ian Matheson
CEO
AUSTRALASIAN IR ASSOCIATION

portfolio of investor engagement. It's not just a matter of setting up a Zoom call occasionally. For the most advanced IR functions, technology has meant vastly greater complexity in terms of audience segmentation—profiling your investment community and mapping the right channel to each investor—so that you are always interacting with your key audiences using the most appropriate medium for them.

A CHANGED TALENT PROFILE

All these pressures—especially regulation, sustainability concerns, and novel investor types—have driven profound shifts in IR's talent base, altering its profile in the process.

That's nothing new: Over 70 years, IR has undergone more image reinventions than almost any other industry, from the press agents of the 1960s to the accountants of the 1990s to the all-round strategists of today. Each time the markets have shifted, so have investors' communication needs—and a surge of new talent has entered IR as a result, reshaping the profession.

THE SELL-SIDE MOVES IN-HOUSE

The most obvious transition in recent years has been the influx of sell-side analysts into IR. As the analyst's role diminished post-MiFID II, so IR has had to fill the vacant capability. It has meant that analyst skills have become integral to IR (making it a match-fit for former analysts) and that IR's influence has increased with the new scope (making it an attractive career landing zone). In many ways, therefore, MiFID II has simply moved the analyst industry in-house. But our IROs were keen to point out the upsides: It has not just meant more workload and role complexity. It has been a vital part of raising the profession's sophistication levels.

THE NEED FOR WIDE OPERATIONAL KNOWLEDGE

Several interviewees also pointed to a more profound diversification—the rise of IROs with neither finance nor communications backgrounds, but instead wider knowledge of the business and sector.

To cover modern sustainability and reputational accountabilities, today's IROs must increasingly have comprehensive knowledge of the company's entire day-to-day operations—the nuts and bolts of life in every department. What an emerging breed of IRO is bringing, therefore, is not disciplinary expertise but industry and company knowledge: Former R&D scientists taking on senior IR roles in pharma; engineers becoming the IROs of manufacturing companies; and investment bankers slipping naturally into IRO positions in financial services.

"The young people coming into the profession nowadays have a variety of backgrounds," said Kay Bommer, of the German IR Society (DIRK). "It's no longer just the guys who studied accountancy in business school. You still get communicators and economists, but also now historians, biochemists, geologists... One of the best IRO graduates we ever had on our IRO accreditation program had studied religion."

It speaks even more firmly to the need for IR globally to come together and decide how to differentiate themselves as members of a skilled discipline with defined capabilities; with universally recognized accreditation; and with a unique skills profile that others can't match.

> The move by sell-side analysts into investor relations has gained pace in recent years, particularly post MiFID II. It can be a steep learning curve to make that move, particularly given the demands of running a financial reporting process for the first time.
>
> *Clara Melia*
> **Founder and CEO**
> **EQUITORY**

POWER IRO–A NEW, SOPHISTICATED IRO

But the drive to give investors a more nuanced company portrait than basic asset acquisition or cost-cutting—and to give the C-Suite more insights to inform strategic decision-making—has altered IR's talent profile in more radical ways.

> Over the last decade the seniority and maturity of the IR managers in my organization has vastly increased. The IR department is recognized in the company as a breeding ground for talent. As such we have no issue attracting top talent from the whole company to further improve their profile during the years they stay with us. Looking back, members of our IR team went on to have attractive next career steps in the company.
>
> *Constantin Fest*
> **SVP/Head of IR**
> **GSK**

Once, the IR role was a proving ground for junior talent. The most common pathway to IRO was via promotion from finance or communications—a young high-performer with a penchant for market analytics and writing. Today, it's too important a role to be trusted to inexperienced talent. Companies are instead parachuting in immensely sophisticated business professionals as IROs—strategists, investment bankers, financial consultants, and tier-1 analysts from the major Wall Street banks.

This new cadre of IR executives has seniority and executive experience. Armed with CFAs, ACAs and MBAs, they bring sophistication and credibility. More than that, they bring ambition.

In the last five years, I have seen record numbers of high-flyers moving into IRO positions—and then often moving out again. No longer a "testing ground" for young talent, it has become a "proof point" for ambitious executives; a springboard to the boardroom. IROs I've helped to appoint in recent years have gone on to become heads of strategy, heads of corporate development, CFOs, even CEOs. On the current trajectory— and with the vast skillset that the role now encompasses—that trend looks likely to continue.

It was 2005 when a sell-side analyst first approached me to get advice about moving onto the IR side. More from the sell-side and investment banking have followed (and in some cases failed!) in the years since, as the profession built a reputation for itself as an interesting place to be at the intersection of finance, strategy, communications and compliance.

And the influx of more financially literate and strategic IROs has continued to encourage others to up their game and ultimately, has been part of elevating the whole profession, the status the IRO is accorded within companies today and the expectations of what good IR looks like.

Karen Keyes
Head of Investor Relations
CANADIAN TIRE CORPORATION

3. IR AROUND THE WORLD

A global profession

W hen the US's National Investor Relations Institute (NIRI) was established in 1969, there was no such thing as a national IR society—because there had never been such a thing as a recognized IR profession. But at the time, a burgeoning cadre of IROs from different corporations spotted that they were no longer alone, and felt compelled to distinguish themselves as a discrete industry with its own professional standards and requirements—and to come together and learn from each other, building a roadmap for the future development of the profession.

Fast forward to today, and we have IR associations established in dozens of countries around the world. We asked some of the heads of these associations to give us a "State of the Nation" view of IR in their particular corner of the globe.

GERMANY

The first time anyone in Germany had ever heard of IR was the mid-'90s, when a small handful of mostly old, middle-aged men (myself included) found themselves with a business card saying "Investor Relations." And they didn't really know what that meant or what was expected of them, so they founded the German IR Society—and began exchanging views and looking abroad to learn what others had done before them. There were probably fewer than ten people in the whole country who considered themselves IR managers back then.

Only with the IPO of Deutsche Telekom in the late '90s did that begin to change, because that was when the idea of owning shares as a private individual was first introduced into Germany—literally. We didn't have an equity culture before that, but the German government decided to enable start-ups to finance themselves via the capital markets.

From then on, the understanding of "What is IR" went through waves in Germany. Initially, it was a lot about marketing— selling that retail investment. There were many companies competing for the available capital, so a lot of it was about adding a rosy tint. (Also because you couldn't study IR at university, so the early folk were all comms people.) Then the Neuer Markt, which had been launched with great fanfare in 1997 as "the European NASDAQ," collapsed in 2002 with the bursting of the dot.com bubble, at which point IR in Germany become more focused on the numbers. We became "the explainer of the equity story, not the seller of the shares," and the economists and number crunchers came into the profession.

Then came the 2008 financial crisis. Regulation got tougher and the legal texts were called things like "The Shareholder Protection Act" not the "Let's Get The Capital Markets Growing Again Act," so it placed a lot of pressure on IR. And regulation has been getting tougher on a daily basis ever since. The eight-page quarterly report? Forget it. They're now 100 pages in some companies. And what you could and couldn't say became increasingly important. So as an IRO, you didn't need to be just good at telling the equity story, you also needed a certain legal expertise to understand the right time to call in legal advisors on what you were doing.

And that was when we, as an association, sat down and said: What are we doing as a profession? We had found out we were not just salespeople—that doesn't build the relationship we need with investors. And nor does knowing the numbers but knowing nothing else. We're not the legal beagles. So what actually is the goal of IR?

That was ten years ago and the answer we came up with was: *"We are here as IROs to add value in decreasing the cost of capital."* That sounds very theoretical but, in reality, that is the ultimate goal of the profession, and it remains our mission as DIRK today: To reduce the cost of capital. And you can do that in many ways: You need to build good relationships. You need to explain the financial figures. You need to understand the legal ramifications of what's happening. And, while you're not the salesperson, you need to get the shares sold by being able to explain the equity story.

So today, as an IRO, you need to be very multi-skilled. In German, we have a phrase—the *eierlegende wollmilchsau*—the "egg-laying, woolly, dairy pig"; an incredible, single animal that can provide you with eggs, milk, wool and meat.

But it's a good sign. That complexity of demand and expectation means that the profession is in robust health here. Our IR community is about 1,200 people. IR in Germany is now very highly regarded—although not as much as in some countries like the US and UK, and the model is different: The US and UK tend to have relatively small IR departments who use brokers a lot. In Germany, most of that work is done in-house by the IRO. But we can do that because IR has professionalized here quite considerably—and, with all humility, we played our part in that. DIRK created and runs the Certified IRO program, a unique certification totally unlike any other national association's diplomas. Ours is a half-year study course and it's very tough—people fail it. But whoever gets through that, we believe is ready to speak to high-level analysts and investors.

Kay Bommer
Managing Director
DIRK - GERMAN IR SOCIETY

HONG KONG

IR is a young profession in Hong Kong. The Hong Kong Investor Relations Association (HKIRA) is celebrating its 15th anniversary, and today it has about 1,300 members, mainly working with Hong-Kong-listed companies.

But the demand for professional and experienced IROs is increasing and the career path of IROs is promising: Hong Kong has been ranked as the world's number one IPO venue seven times in the past 14 years, and is now one of the most sought-after listing venues for new-economy companies, opening novel dimensions for investors and bringing significant impact to the broader capital market in Hong Kong. That growing capital market provides an excellent platform for the IR industry to grow here.

There have been challenges too: The tension between China and the US reduced American investors' interest in China/Hong Kong stocks. Diversification of the shareholder base has therefore become a priority for IROs in China/Hong Kong but, without the support of brokerage houses, it's difficult for IROs (especially young ones) to reach out to new investors.

Also: The poor economy and spiking interest rates have affected the capital market, reducing investors' interest in the stock market. The resulting drop in stock prices has put pressure on IROs; it is getting more difficult for them to justify their performance.

Then there are the practical details: Covid has fundamentally changed a lot of the day-to-day role here. Virtual meetings became the new normal. Having said that, face-to-face meetings with investors are still required as part of the package, since trust and relationships are built more easily through physical touchpoints—but the travel budget to allow for that is now proving difficult to get back in the same way as before.

Eva Chan
Chair
Hong Kong Investor Relations Association

ISRAEL

When we founded the Israeli IR Forum (IIRF), it was very challenging to convince executives in the local capital-market community to join our vision. The Israeli capital market is small, and very few Israeli-listed companies employed IROs, so most people didn't see the value in promoting it as a discipline. Those who did were usually dual-listing companies or companies operating in the global markets.

Over these five years, though, the challenges and emerging situations in both local and global capital markets (e.g., COVID, inflation, Ukraine conflict, climate crisis) have meant that, slowly but surely, comprehension of IR's importance has grown across the Israeli market.

Today, more companies and management teams prioritize IR strategies and methodologies. They invest in efforts to promote IR as a practice and are hiring more in-house IR professionals, some even now broadening their IR management role into an IRO executive position.

But we still have a long way to go. In order to advance both capabilities within and principles of IR, we need to integrate

IR methodologies into advanced business programs in exclusive universities. Because increasingly over the next ten to 20 years, I think IR will inevitably become much more involved in senior-management decisions, leading an IR strategy that is plugged into the organizational strategy and vice versa.

Iris Golani
Founder & Director
Israeli Investor Relations Forum (IIRF)
Israeli Association of Publicly Traded Companies

ITALY

The metamorphosis away from a purely balance-sheet-driven function in Italy has happened: At senior level in large caps, IROs have become representatives of the institution. They not only "sell" the equity and bond story, but they bring together all stakeholders to help them understand what the company is really about from a strategic point of view.

But although the situation has improved, an IRO in Italy is still categorized as "Tier 2" management: It is seen as a transitory position on the corporate ladder; a position of significance but not one that has realized the financial and hierarchical status of top management. At the same time, many IROs struggle to find exit positions outside of IR, so this is a Catch-22. Career progression for IROs in Italy remains challenging and statistical research shows that remuneration for Italian IROs is lower than in the rest of Europe.

As a result, I feel the average competency of Italian IROs could be higher, if only in order to attract and retain better talent across the profession: Talented people, especially junior resources, often opt to leave for other opportunities. There are reasons to hope for better in the future, although that hope will only become concrete with proof: The future of the profession depends a great deal on whether IROs are truly able to demonstrate that they can bring additional value to their company—and to do that, we need to think laterally.

For example, if we take the IR unit of a bank, on top of the "usual suspects" (stock price and credit ratings) the institution would benefit from many interventions that IR could directly influence: Lower cost of debt and bank financing; lower cost of equity issuance; lower cost of insurance providers (both for traditional and ESG-related risks); investment-banking fees, should the IR unit pitch for an IPO along with; investment-banking fees (equity and bond sales), should the IR unit educate banking clients' approach to IR; lower cost of potential sanctions related to a poor approach to financial communication; and so on.

These sorts of true value-adds—proactive attention to and involvement in what really matters to the company's commercial success—could be what makes the difference, and realize the dream of there being a career pathway from IRO to CEO.

As a long-term goal (as a former representative of the Italian IR association), that would be my dream: A former head of IR becoming group CEO. Building the value points above could be what makes that difference.

Piero Munari – Co-Founder - Arwin&Partners
& Former Chair
ITALIAN INVESTOR RELATIONS SOCIETY

SPAIN

The average capability level among our IR professionals is strong, clearly above what you would expect from a smaller market like ours (as shown every year with our above-average success in the most esteemed awards, such as Extel and IR Magazine/IR Impact).

But while we have some of the best, most senior IR professionals in Europe—highly valued by global stakeholders, with significant expertise and a great strategic view—at the same time, we've begun to spot a future talent risk for the function emerging over the last five to seven years in Iberia. It is a generational shortfall: Fewer younger IR professionals are following the strategic pathway that has been carved out by the vanguard, because young talent is usually coming into the profession to perform less strategic roles (i.e., they are more "analyst" positions).

So there is a real risk that the gains we have made over the last few decades now gets lost, because we're not developing talent within the IR profession towards growing into strategic leadership.

Javier Rodriguez-Vega
Managing Director
The Spanish Association for Investor Relations (AERI)

MIDDLE EAST

The spotlight is now very much on the Middle East, with five of our ten markets on international emerging-market (EM) indices, and the largest boasting a market capitalization of nearly USD3 trillion—making it now one of the largest stock markets in the world. And with a burgeoning IPO pipeline across both state and private sectors, what's not to like?

The market's appetite for the larger regional companies is reflected in the increased EM index weightings. We're also seeing more IR enquiries and a concerted response by both the companies and the exchanges they're listed on. Indeed, we have listed stock exchanges in the region leading by example too. The MSX launched a Dividend Policy for its listed companies aiming to ensure clear and transparent communication between issuers and capital markets about dividend payout. The GCC exchanges have featured in international roadshows in both the USA and UK. Asia next perhaps, where there is also investor appetite. In addition, there is a natural affinity with Islamic finance— in Southeast Asia, for example, where there are some useful parallels to capitalize on. And why not, with all to play for in international capital markets?

Naturally, ESG is increasingly bubbling to the surface in statutory reporting requirements. Though not mandated across our regional markets, individual stock exchanges are working together to establish a common baseline of ESG metrics against which listed companies can be assessed by stakeholders. As a result, while we're only in the early stages of integrating ESG thinking into business strategy and reporting, we expect listed companies here to be in a stronger position soon to address these broader stakeholder needs. MEIRA is well positioned to support IROs and Issuers with their increasing ESG & Sustainability requirements, having recently developed the ESG CIRO, an introductory Certificate providing ESG foundations for investor relations officers, launching in Q2 2025.

This is already happening to some extent among larger companies, particularly those in financial services or higher impact sectors (e.g., energy). There will be a natural trickle-down to the next tier as the competition for attention and capital drives a need to differentiate their investment stories. That in turn will demand greater prioritization of resources for the collection, analysis and presentation of material data as part of running a sustainable business. Nothing new in that—just a mindset switch towards what external stakeholders want to see for investment, as opposed to just what management and the Board need. Indeed, many companies recognize this and are beginning to do it. Now for the formal reporting part!

Having over 200 Certified IROs (CIROs, based on the prevalent UK CIR) in the Middle East—so roughly 10% of the worldwide total—where do we go next?

First, with well over 1,000 listed companies in the region, we have plenty more IROs to get through the CIRO program. The growing regional IPO pipeline only increases the demand for more qualified IR practitioners.

Second, having completed the CIRO, what is the natural aspiration for our more senior IROs? Currently, few go to the C-suite or Board—though those routes are possible. Yet, given their proximity to the executive team and the Board, why not more encouragement towards non-executive roles for those wanting to continue to make a difference to business? MEIRA works closely with the GCC Board Directors Institute because, we believe, it's a partnership that promotes exactly that type of professional development thinking in our IR community. The region needs more qualified directors. Competent IROs certainly bring considerable transferable skills and much needed capital market experience in advising senior people to get it right. Onwards and upwards, IROs, your time will come!

Paolo Casamassima & *John Gollifer* (Current and former)
Chief Executive Officer
MEIRA (THE MIDDLE EAST IR ASSOCIATION)

THE NETHERLANDS

The Netherlands Association for Investor Relations (NEVIR) is doing well—healthy both financially and in membership numbers, especially following an influx of new joiners post-Covid. We now have two-thirds of all listed companies in Amsterdam represented in the association.

What have been the main drivers of that growth? First, a simple desire to extend collaboration and problem solving outside of the narrow limits of one's own organization: In most Dutch companies, the IR function is very small—perhaps two or three employees. So to have the opportunity to come out and meet a wider IR community and be able to share some of the successes (or frustrations) that you experience in your day-to-day job, is something that is appreciated. People are especially looking for fewer presentations from consultants around key issues (AGMs, EU taxonomy, or whatever is topical) and are asking more for in-depth, peer conversation around these specific problems—meeting in small forums and having detailed discussions on what matters.

Many of the issues our members face are universal; others are recognizably northwest European. ESG, for example, plays a bigger role in the Netherlands than in most countries worldwide (and is certainly more of a priority for our IR community than those in Brazil, South Africa or the US, for example) but it's not significantly different than in the UK or Germany.

What we see a real hunger for right now, in terms of best practices, is a clearer understanding of "What does good look like?"—because that is something that the profession really lacks on a universal level.

How do you do good targeting? How do you manage increased reporting requirements? How do you manage the drop-off in sell-side research? What exactly is "best in class"? There is no really clear definition of that, especially given all the changes to the role in recent times. So there is a real desire to come out and talk to each other; to truly share "This is how we do it" and ask "How do you do it?". It speaks to a real desire for more professionalism within IR communities.

Andreas Bork
Former Chair of the Board
The Netherlands Association for IR (NEVIR)

ROMANIA

As we speak, Romania is celebrating the monumental success of its capital market, with Hidroelectrica (H2O), the country's largest and most profitable local company and a leading hydropower energy producer, listing on the Bucharest Stock Exchange after an astounding EUR 1.9 billion IPO.

This remarkable achievement reflects the tremendous efforts of our country's investor relations (IR) teams, who have diligently promoted the market and attracted global investors to Romania. During the momentous ring-the-bell ceremony, many speakers acknowledged this accomplishment, describing it as a "graduation ceremony": The Romanian market now boasts a market capitalization surpassing Prague and Budapest markets for the first time, placing it just behind Poland.

As President of the Romanian IR Association (ARIR) and an IR consultant, I've had the privilege of witnessing this historic moment first hand. Hidroelectrica (H2O), a founding member of ARIR, was among the 11 members that joined me in 2018 to establish an organization dedicated to promoting IR best practices. Our belief in adhering to standards of transparency, corporate governance, and proactive communication with investors has borne fruit: Today, ARIR boasts nearly 40 members, comprising not only the largest listed companies but also smaller and junior market-listed ones. Over the years, we have hosted countless hours of streamed content and events, gathered thousands of media mentions, and fostered a vibrant community through networking events.

At the outset (when I was serving as the IRO of the Bucharest Stock Exchange), ARIR was met with skepticism by some members of the local investor community. With many companies listed for 20+ years, they thought the ways they communicated with the market couldn't be altered. Looking back, it's difficult to pinpoint a single factor that contributed to the enhanced awareness of IR that has resulted but by bringing together IROs, encouraging them to exchange ideas and celebrate achievements, we motivated others to join our cause.

It also speaks to the incredible growth in the profession in Romania recently. I initially learned IR as a practitioner in 2010, and back then the profession was small and the terminology seemed bewildering. However, with the advent of ARIR, we managed to have the IR profession officially recognized in the occupational registry in Romania in 2023, providing clarity regarding the role of directors and specialists within companies.

And now much more than that: Imagine if your company received an annual rating on how effectively it communicated with investors. For listed companies in Bucharest, that has been the reality for the past five years. Every year, ARIR evaluates listed companies using a methodology outlined on our website, allowing them to receive up to ten points. The final rating is then displayed on the Bucharest Stock Exchange website for each company.

Starting with only three companies achieving a perfect score of ten in 2019, this number has now increased to 16. The methodology is modified annually by a committee comprising investors and analysts. This year, the focus has been on elements like quarterly conference calls, presentations, recordings, transcripts, translations and Excel. With numerous challenges arising each year, investors expect swift access to comparable and easily digestible data.

Today the IR talent market in Romania is fluid, flexible and in high demand. The surge in listings 2020-2021 led to a migration of IR professionals between companies and increased calls for external assistance from experienced IROs; as a consequence, consultancy services have rapidly expanded.

Looking ahead, we anticipate several challenges for IR professionals in the coming years: The rise of AI necessitating integration of big data analysis into our activities; the need to develop strong digitization competencies; the complexity of stakeholder engagement requiring enhanced soft skills; and sharpened leadership abilities to position IR as a strategic function within the company.

By addressing these challenges head-on, we are confident that the IR profession in Romania will continue to thrive and play a vital role in the growth and development of businesses across the country.

Daniela Maior (Serban)
President & Co-Founder
Romanian Investor Relations Association

SOUTH AFRICA

Regretfully, the IR profession in South Africa has not evolved meaningfully enough over the last 20 years, and the value of an effective IR function in ensuring a fair share price for a company is—more often than not—still underestimated by C-Suite and boards here. While a few listed corporates have embraced the opportunities presented by an effective IRO, these examples are quite isolated, not representative of a general market change.

But while corporates have not evolved enough in their views of IR, we're slowly seeing other market players—such as the buy- and sell-side—demand more, and with this their perception of the value of the IR function has increased. The market changes have therefore improved the profile and potential reputation of the IR function and certainly offer opportunity for the function to make a difference. The market changes are, in part, because the buy- and sell-side function itself has changed, with the onset of regulatory changes such as MiFID and with the step change in the way people communicate following COVID-19.

Some of the challenges IROs face in South Africa are directly linked to the ineffectiveness of the function, itself due to a lack of best practice and mentoring. This is the rock on which the IR Society of South Africa is being built.

So there is a lot to do to improve management's perceptions—and the market's expectations—of IROs. Education is needed of the IROs themselves, the companies they serve, as well as the capital markets generally: Best-practice sharing, networking and capital markets-training to understand the importance of proper communication.

Debbie Millar
Chair
IR Society of South Africa

UK

The IR Society was established over 40 years ago and our mission remains to promote best practice in investor relations; to support the professional development of our members; to represent their views to regulatory bodies, the investment community and government; and to act as a forum for issuers and the investment community.

As the UK's IR community and industry have grown over the last four decades, the IR Society has grown to a membership base of over 850 IR practitioners and has responded to the changing market dynamics, through our work across policy and best practice, professional development, events and networking and mentoring, among our other activities.

During that time, we have seen the IR profession and community evolve immensely in the UK. While the administrative aspect is still vital at some level within the IR team, today financial acumen and strategic communication skills are now essential, with the IRO being uniquely positioned as a trusted advisor to the C-Suite, other key internal stakeholders, and at the heart of the development of corporate strategy.

There are, however, some challenges specific to the UK capital market and IROs, as we encounter significant de-equitization and a decline in company listings. Regulatory change and reforms are needed in order to restore growth and competitiveness in the UK, and London can be restored as an attractive listing destination. In addition, innovation in IR is rapid across the globe and the IRO will need to work in harmony with, and understand, the impact of technological changes including the growth of AI. For the IRO, this is still at a nascent stage, still under experimentation where best practice can't yet necessarily be defined, and AI will never be able to replace the human relationship element (so important in the IR role). But what it will do is enable us to work smarter and more efficiently. IR will need to evolve and embrace technological change in the future, while remembering the IR Society's core values of professionalism, excellence, integrity, and transparency.

Laura Hayter
CEO
The Investor Relations Society, UK

USA

The IR profession has undergone a number of changes, disrupted by external and other challenges, and continues to evolve, and IR professionals have to remain abreast of that evolution. So, as the steward of the IR profession in the US, NIRI: The Association for Investor Relations takes a leadership role in identifying its scope and implications.

NIRI also proactively recommends practitioners and those who serve the profession—including NIRI—how to plan for and adapt to these ongoing changes through our NIRI Think Tank projects and research program. The first Think Tank report, *The Disruption Opportunity: the Future of Investor Relations,* was published in 2019 in conjunction with the 50th anniversary of NIRI's founding. Based on the collective conclusions of a diverse committee of 12 industry thought leaders, poring over the results of a survey of 181 NIRI members, it was an exploration of the primary forces driving change within the IR profession, as well as potential pathways to ensure continued relevance and professional success.

These included the changing nature of investors, capital markets, structural and technological change, and the expanding knowledge and competencies required in IR. Subsequent Think Tanks have explored artificial intelligence in IR, and corporate purpose.

In terms of the overall state of IR, our most recent study of the profession and compensation trends in North America reinforced the high value of investor relations. Key findings included:

> IR has become more essential given that capital markets are increasingly complex, more highly regulated, and demand more disclosure and transparency.

> IR is a very desirable career path, continuing trends highlighted in previous surveys: More report that the position has been elevated within their companies; fewer report IR roles as rotational; and more report a desire to remain permanently in the IR field.

> More than 90% of IR professionals are increasingly optimistic about the future of the profession.

> IR is "pandemic proof" as evidenced by the recent significant increase in compensation levels.

> In an increasingly credentialed profession, NIRI's Investor Relations Charter® (IRC) is the top credential of senior-level US IROs.

In a dynamic and evolving profession shaped by a variety of external and internal influences, there is no more exciting and important time to be an investor relations professional than today.

Matt Brusch
President and CEO
NIRI: The Association for Investor Relations

4. OUR CHALLENGES

The mountains to climb

CHOPPY WATERS AHEAD

In 2019, the National Investor Relations Institute (NIRI), the United States professional association for investor relations professionals, surveyed its members about the future: What did they see coming down the line? What was going to disrupt the industry? What did the future hold? The results underscore the challenges our profession faces.

The overall consensus of *The Disruption Opportunity: the Future of Investor Relations* was that IR is at a true inflection point, from where it must now begin to evolve rapidly to meet the changing environment—otherwise it risks becoming "a low-value, tactical function." With the pace of these changes increasing, the research concluded that it was of the utmost urgency for the industry to come together to chart a successful path forward.

The most pressing issues the think tank identified included:

> the changing nature of investors, notably the rise of indexing and passive investing, and the decline of active management;
> increasing shareholder activism;
> growth of ESG investing and demand for ESG disclosures;
> increasing reliance by private companies on private equity funding and M&A, and the resulting decline in the number of public companies;
> the transition to quantitative/algorithmic driven trading;
> the growth of data analytics/artificial intelligence; and
> MiFID II and the decline of the sell-side.

In our own interviews with IROs and industry experts around the world, many of these same issues came back again and again—five years on, and it seems we are still stuck in many of the same muddy holes.

Here we look at the four most commonly cited issues by our interviewees: Investor activism; the decline in publicly listed companies; the rise of passive investing; and the need to "level up" the profession in areas where it is still immature.

> IR is at a cross-roads—all skilled up with not as many places to go. With increased emphasis on data-led passive investment, more opacity in the drivers of share price movement, sparser and AI-driven financial-media coverage, fewer sell-side analysts covering companies, and regulators losing some of their authority, it is harder for IROs to point to "wins" or to know where to prioritize. Added to which, there are more consultants, investment bankers and lawyers vying for management attention on the road to shareholder value creation and stakeholder management.
>
> A good IRO has advantages though—their inside knowledge of the company, its business model and its strategy, plus a unique understanding of how to communicate with the investor audience, and the ability to do it.
>
> *Karen Keyes*
> Head of Investor Relations
> CANADIAN TIRE CORPORATION

THE ACTIVIST SURGE

Investor activism is nothing new. The Securities and Exchange Commission (SEC) was formed in response to activist calls for shareholder rights in the wake of the 1929 Wall Street Crash. The 1970s brought socially oriented activism, the 1980s corporate-governance and executive-pay activism, and the 1990s environmental activism.

But what we're seeing now is of another order of magnitude: The industrialization of investor power grabs and pressure pushes.

The campaign by US short-seller Hindenburg Research against India's Adani Group in January 2023 wiped $108bn off the company's market value in a matter of days, crashing the fortunes of billionaire founder Gautam Adani.

It was the latest artillery barrage in a mounting war of control. In 2022, almost 1,000 companies were targeted by new activist campaigns. In Q1 2023 alone, 69 new campaigns were started globally, the second-highest quarter of activity since 2019 (source: Lazard Capital Markets Advisory).

> The most immediate challenge for IR is the rise of shareholder activism. Keeping the Board and management abreast of likely activism, as well as their demands, should be top of mind for IR professionals. No company is immune. And shareholder activism is not always a threat—it may pose an opportunity to hone the investment proposition, end inertia and unlock value that would otherwise be trapped in inefficient ways of working and legacy thought processes.
>
> *Nikki Catrakilis-Wagner*
> **Director of IR**
> **TIGER BRANDS**

> Investors today expect more transparency, especially at times of market volatility. For example, during COVID, we needed to provide them with real-time liquidity/cash flow data to calm their fears. As a result, the IRO of today needs to be much more mindful of—and therefore be prepared for—potential activists.
>
> *Ashish Kohli*
> **VP Investor Relations**
> **GENERAL MOTORS**

THE PROVABLE IMPORTANCE OF THE IRO

But all of this has further underlined the importance of investor relations, further strengthening the profession's development.

Empirical research[3] in *The Accounting Review* in 2022, for example, showed IR engagement as being positively correlated with not just increased investor confidence in management and the board (as measured by approval for board members on shareholder votes), but a lower likelihood of activism.

Specifically, having an IRO correlated with a 20-40% lower likelihood of a tender offer and a 10-20% lower likelihood of a 13-D filing (indicating at least 5% ownership and an intent to influence management). Among firms that did experience an activist campaign, those with robust IR engagement had provably less costly and contentious campaigns—and lower likelihoods of CEO turnover—than those without it.

> Perhaps the most important development in recent years has been the rise of activist investors. Never has it been so important to understand the hopes and fears of everyone on the shareholder register. The IRO has become, again, the first line of defense in detecting and pre-empting potential activist attacks. In the past, the IR function used to be regarded as a cost item by many companies. Today, with activist attacks on companies all round the world, the IR function has come to be seen as an indispensable insurance policy.
>
> *Matthew O'Keeffe*
> **Managing Director**
> **FTI CONSULTING**

---

[3] Chapman, Kimball L., et al. 'Investor relations, engagement, and shareholder activism.' *The Accounting Review* 97.2 (2022): 77-106.

Crucially, it also found the stabilizing effect of great IR on activism increases incrementally with the tenure of the IRO: In short, the more established their relationship with an IRO, the lower the likelihood of shareholders launching campaigns against a firm's management.

In other words: Experienced IROs provably head off shareholder activism.

THE DECLINE IN PUBLICLY LISTED COMPANIES

In 1996, there were 8,090 listed companies in the US. By Q1 2023, that had fallen to 4,572—a drop of over 43%. Meanwhile, the number quoted on the London Stock Exchange has almost halved in 20 years, and just 34 companies were publicly listed in Europe in the first half of 2023—the lowest level since 2009.[4] Even JP Morgan's Jamie Dimon is worried—in his 2024 shareholder letter he laments "the total should have grown dramatically, not shrunk."

The reasons for this are legion and well-documented, particularly increasing reliance on M&A and private-equity funding to raise capital, and mandatory reporting requirements (and their significant fixed costs) leading to a reduction in IPOs.

---

[4] 'European IPOs fall to lowest level since 2009,' *Financial Times*, 2 August 2023

But recent research[5] analyzing all these factors—the number of publicly listed companies, aggregate economic conditions, M&A activity and private-equity investments—in 51 countries worldwide showed that by far the biggest statistically attributable reason for the decline has been regulation—in particular Sarbanes-Oxley (2002).

U.S. LISTED COMPANIES

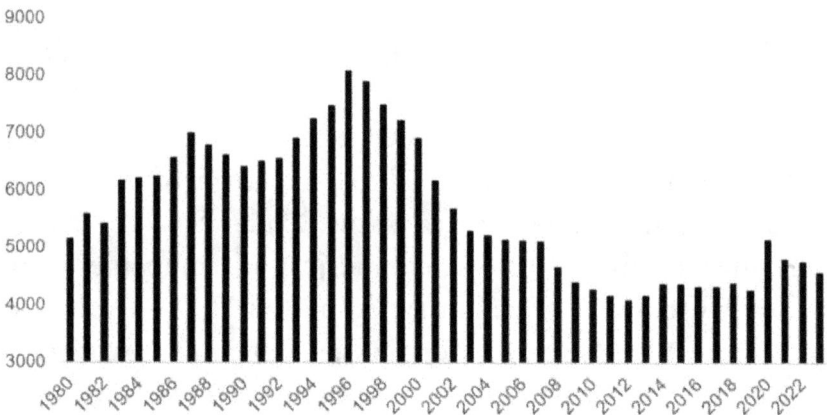

Source: World Bank and Statista

What are the implications for IR? Increased competition for investor attention among a limited set of firms means the talent market is that much tighter, with a declining number of vacant positions and an overcrowded talent pool. To rise to the very top, you have to have something provably better than the rest.

---

[5] Lattanzio, Gabriele, William L. Megginson, and Ali Sanati. 'Dissecting the listing gap: Mergers, private equity, or regulation?' *Journal of Financial Markets* (2023): 100836.

https://papers.ssrn.com/sol3/papers.cfm?abstract_id=3329555

In terms of the day-to-day role, the implications are more profound—the need for better targeting, with perhaps a more concentrated group of institutional investors; and, facing a decrease in the frequency of IPOs, IR professionals will need to focus more on building deep relationships with investors by tailoring communication that aligns with those investors' long-term goals.

As more companies opt to stay private, might IR professionals also need to adapt—to engage with private equity firms and institutional investors in private markets; building relationships and communicating effectively in a different environment? Will the IRO role in many organizations morph into "Private Equity Officer"?

Over the next 10 years the number of publicly traded companies will:

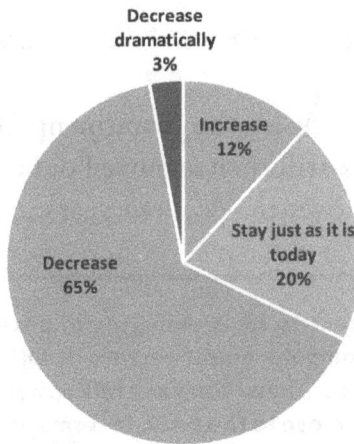

NIRI's survey of 181 North American IROs (2019)—two-thirds believe the number of listed companies will decrease this decade

Whatever happens, it looks like a trend that is here to stay—and nobody has a clear answer to the problem yet.

Small and mid-sized companies are delisting because it's simply not worth the effort: the regulatory burden of listing is increasing (which adds cost), and the low volumes traded on stock exchanges mean it's not as effective an ownership structure as it used to be. So companies are actively looking for a private equity partner that can delist them. Not only do I see that trend continuing, I see it accelerating as the pressure for more transparency produces increasing regulation.

What does that mean for the IR profession? Fewer listed companies but potentially slightly more IROs per listed company, because the job is becoming more complex. So my guess is that, overall, the size of the profession will remain reasonably constant. But that's a guess. In Amsterdam they're worried about it, London is worried about it. We hear it again and again when we are talking to investors.

Andreas Bork
Vice-President, IR & ESG
SHELL

THE RISE OF PASSIVE INVESTING

According to research by the Investment Company Institute (ICI), more than $2 trillion has moved out of active funds and into passive funds over the past ten years in the US alone.

An existential threat to IR is emerging in passive funds. There is no point in a company employing an IR Officer if its biggest investors are all algorithms. You can't talk to a robot. My personal view is that we are close to the peak, in terms of the proportion of listed companies owned by passive funds, so my hope is that the passive threat will recede over time. But I might be quite wrong about this of course.

Matthew O'Keeffe
Managing Director
FTI CONSULTING

Passive funds now hold a higher percentage of the US stock market than active funds—by mid-year 2023, according to data compiled by Bloomberg, they accounted for half of all assets in US mutual funds and Exchange Traded Funds (ETFs), up from 47% in 2022 and 44% in 2021.

It has fundamentally changed the shape of IR as a discipline. With so many passive investors non-human, they are not interested in the quarterly communications cycle, don't listen to conference calls, meet with management teams, attend conferences, or speak with sell-side analysts.

HOW WE RESPOND

So how should IROs be responding, and what does it mean for the future of the profession?

The first demand it places on IR is to understand the metrics passive investors are using to evaluate their portfolio companies' governance structures and voting guidelines—then to make sure your company's metrics match them.

Successful IR requires the continued engagement of the buy-side in the active fund-management industry. The biggest structural threats to active and effective IR are the growth in passive investment strategies and the declining number of listed companies.

Clara Melia
Founder and CEO
EQUITORY

It also requires that you be familiar with the variety of indexes that include your stock, and aware of key items that could influence inclusion (such as market capitalization or dividend policy), to ensure you don't suffer an automated exclusion from a particular index for a remediable issue.

Finally, it means monitoring third-party data about your company's metrics, so the correct financial information is presented on popular financial platforms, and your company's stock is adequately screened for. Truly it has never been more important for companies to create financial metrics that are standardized and comparable across companies: It could be the difference between having a robust and vibrant portfolio of investors—and that shareholder base suddenly falling off a cliff one day without warning.

Unlike those who think IR is on the downturn and with AI you won't need IR, or with passive investors you don't need IR—the opposite is true. You need to make sure you talk to the right people, and put the right thought into it—so that you become a member of the right indices and then the passive investors will have to buy you.

Kay Bommer
Managing Director
GERMAN IR SOCIETY (DIRK)

The future? Investors, markets and regulations are all constantly evolving, so the IR profession will have to keep pushing itself to raise its level constantly if it is to thrive—not just thinking about how to use IR leadership as a stepping stone to becoming CFO or head of strategy, but how to ensure that senior IR professionals are themselves increasingly considered management.

Javier Rodriguez-Vega
Managing Director
SPANISH ASSOCIATION FOR IR (AERI)

LEVELLING UP THE PROFESSION WORLDWIDE

As our research shows, the top tier of IROs are already operating at leadership level, particularly in large-cap companies in major markets.

But that is not a universal picture globally: In smaller companies and up-and-coming regions, the function is still going through the familiar teething problems—junior teams (or IR support bought on the market), a lack of strategic expertise, poor boardroom visibility and low levels of access. This was

---

The current state of IR? I think we still have a long way to go. First, to realise our best future requires a corporate culture (embodied by a sophisticated CEO and Board) that understands the IR role. For too many IROs who show genuine promise, that basic context is lacking: You find impressive IROs who are not appreciated by colleagues or stakeholders because their own ExCos/Boards don't understand their role. As a result, the IRO doesn't get the tools and environment they need, they struggle to make an impact, and the lack of value becomes a self-fulfilling prophecy.

What does a positive environment look like? A CEO who regularly asks the IRO "How would the market react if...?" and who makes them part of the executive committee. And Boards who feel compelled to get market feedback directly from the IRO, interested in her/his view before making a strategic decision.

But as IR leaders, we also have a responsibility here to improve ourselves and earn that right. We need to be brave enough to leave our comfort zone, manage uncertainty, take risks, and continuously train ourselves so that we are prepared to take on new responsibilities when those opportunities arise.

Juan Gaitan
Director of Investor Relations
CELLNEX TELECOM

---

noticeably the judgement of those in less mature markets. To create a truly international discipline, we all have a part to play in raising standards everywhere.

It mirrors what we see in executive search at Broome Yasar and PLBsearch: The US market—the profession's birthplace— is still the most consistently advanced in terms of executive IRO talent and their strategic prominence inside companies. Several European countries (notably the UK and Germany) today come very close, and certainly the best IROs in these countries are on a par with their transatlantic counterparts.

Asia, Africa, the Middle East and South America, in different ways, are still developmental, and the state of the IR profession broadly reflects the maturity of those financial markets— catching up fast but still with leadership status for IROs varying greatly from company to company. Many interviewees in these regions landed on the same key improvement point—the need for greater education of management on the unique advantages IR can bring, if given the opportunity to flourish.

THE NEED TO PROFESSIONALIZE

Ultimately, our IROs and association heads recognized that, to be surmounted, these hurdles needed a capability uplift within the profession—a step-change not just in the competencies but in the strategic outlook and value-adding focus of IROs themselves.

To achieve that, we need to become a recognized global profession rather than a disparate collection of talented leaders. We need to define ourselves as a unique and specific discipline, with parameters that apply globally, with training and education of the next generation according to universal best practices. That means accreditation and certification. Getting everyone stepping up to the next level. It is not just important because it builds on the gains made. It's about safeguarding IR's future and drawing more people into its talent pipeline.

ACCREDITATION AND CERTIFICATION PROGRAMS AROUND THE WORLD

Many national IR associations have been leading this charge for decades. Here, we share some of the qualifications, certification programs and competency frameworks that have been developed around the world by IR societies and institutes.

In 2006 we developed the first IR qualification—the Certificate in Investor Relations (CIR®). The CIR is a valuable benchmark for those already in the profession and an essential prerequisite for those seeking to work in investor relations. The CIR is also widely recognized in those international markets that look to the UK for best-practice principles in regulation and disclosure. Today we are proud to have over 2,500 successful CIR candidates from over 26 countries who have demonstrated their expertise as IR practitioners and enhanced their career development.

Those looking to build on this can undertake our Diploma in IR (DipIR®), which certifies those showing a profound understanding and practical application of the IR skills, tools and expertise needed to become leaders in our profession. Meanwhile, our fast track leadership program, "Deliver," supports high-potential IROs who are seeking the next step up in their career.

Laura Hayter
CEO
THE IR SOCIETY, UK

- ### *USA: INVESTOR RELATIONS CHARTER (IRC) AND THE IR COMPETENCY FRAMEWORK*

For US investor relations professionals, NIRI has been offering the Investor Relations Charter (IRC)® since 2015. The IRC is a certification for established IROs (six years'+ experience), requiring 100 hours of study and the passing of a rigorous exam. Certification is time-limited: To retain credentialed, you must commit to lifelong professional development and maintain continued competence.

Based on its work constantly refreshing the assessment competencies, NIRI has also published an "IR Competency Framework"—freely-available for IROs globally, to download and help you build the skills of your team.

https://www.niri.org/certification
https://www.niri.org/resources/publications/ir-competency-framework

---

To be trusted strategic advisors, IR professionals need not only extensive experience, but also an in-depth understanding of the 'knowledge domains' underlying the profession. At NIRI, we periodically undertake a formal 'Job Task Analysis' study of the profession as part of our IRC credentialing program and have codified and summarized these knowledge domains in the 'IR Competency Framework'—available to all.

Matt Brusch
President and CEO
NIRI: The Association for Investor Relations

- **CANADA: CERTIFIED PROFESSIONAL IN INVESTOR RELATIONS (CPIR)**

This intensive ten-month program (including five days of in-person classroom study), in partnership with top-ranking business school the Rotman School of Management, covers various aspects of IR, including disclosure, regulatory compliance, financial reporting, and communication skills.

https://ciri.org/

- **UK: THE CIR AND THE DIPIR**

The UK's Investor Relations Society was the vanguard of industry accreditation programs, and its CIR and DipIR remain—in global terms—the leading credentials in the industry. The CIR course is a self-learning program, with all of the content necessary for passing the certification exam included in the association's study guide. Applicants are also invited to attend several optional seminars, such as "Demystifying company accounts" and "IR regulation and compliance essentials."

https://irsociety.org.uk/professional-development

- **MIDDLE EAST: CERTIFIED INVESTOR RELATIONS OFFICER PROGRAM (CIRO):**

Delivered in partnership with the UK IR Society and co-certified by them, the Certified Investor Relations Officer (CIRO) program is strongly based on the CIR—around

40 hours of self-directed study followed by an exam—but with elements of Middle East/North Africa-specific content folded into it.

Developed by John Gollifer (who, in an earlier life with the UK IR Society, was instrumental in setting up the CIR), this professional development program aims to provide IR practitioners across the Middle East and North Africa with an up-to-date understanding of the international standards of the profession.

https://meira.me/training/ciro/

- **GERMANY: CERTIFIED INVESTOR RELATIONS OFFICER (CIRO) PROGRAM**

Launched in 2001, this part-time course for German-speaking IROs run by the German investor relations association (DIRK) has a modular structure and is carried out in collaboration with the Frankfurt School of Finance & Management in Frankfurt am Main.

Students spend six months studying part-time through on-the-job learning, online tests and five two-day lecture sessions. After that, there are two exams—one written, one oral—to pass.

https://www.dirk.org/bildungsangebot/ciro-studium

- **AUSTRALASIA: DIPLOMA OF INVESTOR RELATIONS**

A three-day, in-person course, followed by a one-hour online exam, the Diploma of Investor Relations is offered by the Australasian Investor Relations Association (AIRA) to both new and established IR professionals. Day One is specifically designed as a stand-alone course for those recently appointed to their first IR role. Days Two and Three have been developed as an intensive course for experienced investor relations professionals or individuals who have completed Day One as a standalone course.

https://www.australasianir.com.au

5. OUR FUTURE

Future opportunities?

A FUTURE FULL OF REINVENTION

In 2021, the *Harvard Business Review* published a provocative article, 'The Changing Role of the Investor Relations Officer,' presenting a direct challenge to CEOs to radically rethink the role of IRO.

"With investor activism increasing and world markets gripped by uncertainty," it said, "CEOs must empower the IRO to be a proactive leader, building constructive relationships throughout the shareholder base to help the company mitigate various risks. They need to give the IRO a clear mandate to quarterback investor dialogue and get buy-in around all of the elements of management's long-term strategy.

"The IRO must be part of a unified Board and C-Suite investor planning group, and their responsibilities should include building and sustaining credibility with long-term investors, and providing useful information on a timely basis."

I could not agree more. But while in recent years we have seen corporations increasingly waking up to this need, empowering their IRO to play a more substantial role in shaping and molding investor dynamics, the exact nature of a more executive, all-encompassing role could vary between many different possible futures.

Five to ten years from now, will we see an IRO whose role is indistinguishable from that of the corporate affairs director today—responsible for air-traffic-controlling all the swirling vectors that might impact the company's reputation?

Will ESG continue to grow in importance to such an extent that the IRO will be, in effect, the company's primary sustainability risk manager?

Or will the continued rise of the activist investor—and continued competition in the markets—make company financing so volatile and precarious that pure investor relations becomes an executive role in its own right?

In this chapter, we look at some of the possible routes the profession might follow.

"EXECUTIVE IRO"?

If every corporate function that felt it deserved a "seat at the table" got its wish, the boardroom would need to be turned into an auditorium. The pyramid of power ends in a sharp point because it must: Unless final authority rests with a handful of people, either tough decisions aren't made or everyone has too much plausible deniability when they are.

But access is truly essential to a function like IR, whose success is entirely dependent on having a firm grasp of the company story to provide useful, accurate and legally compliant investor information. And being heard in the boardroom means a business plan being built with the best available judgements about their future impact.

So what sort of relationship with the C-Suite is IR moving towards?

Some corporate functions have an engraved nameplate on a seat in every boardroom—the heads of sales, marketing, finance, legal and operations; today, commonly IT and HR too.

But the precise job titles on the ExCo vary in as many combinations as there are companies; the corresponding spheres of accountability for those executives (and how they are arranged into an executive team) are not according to any "standard" but a reflection of the company's business, its culture, its sector, the CEO's personal preferences, the strategic priorities, and more besides. There is no one model.

The extent to which IR ends up on the executive team, therefore, is heavily situation-contingent. What is clear is that the reputation of today's best IROs has given the profession C-Suite credibility like never before. And the reporting compliance buck that now stops with the ExCo and Board has naturally brought IR inside those paneled walls more and more frequently.

The strategic vision of successful IROs, plus their deep knowledge of industry trends and investor expectations, are becoming invaluable in helping companies make key business decisions. So I think IR will (and should) sit at the top table simply because IROs offer insight into market dynamics, competitor issues and investor expectations that nobody else can. But whether or not they report to them, IROs need to have a great relationship with both the CEO and CFO. Gaining their trust and confidence is the most critical element in the function being successful in steering company communications in the right direction.

Ashish Kohli
VP Investor Relations
GENERAL MOTORS

Then there is the emerging desire among CEOs to have, in today's extremely complex and volatile public sphere, a "reputation guardian" sitting on their management team—a hub leader with 360° sight across all reputation-contingent ecosystems (sustainability, brand, media coverage, consumer profile, investors, regulators, government), who can monitor and report the company's standing accurately, and input into strategy on that basis.

Today, that expanded role is increasingly a powerful head of corporate affairs. But it is not impossible to imagine scenarios where, for investment-centric companies and CEOs, the IRO is seen as the natural owner of that role. We have even been seeing IROs being promoted into an all-encompassing corporate affairs role on that basis (See Informa case study, sidebox).

But most of our interviewees were clear: Hierarchy is not as important as presence and influence. It matters less whether the IRO is an official member of the management team than that they have a very close relationship with its members—especially the CFO and CEO. Several argued that, in many ways, an "outside in" vantage allows IR the best of all worlds: Input, while retaining the independence to be the impartial representative of investors.

> If the question is, "Will IR be on executive teams?" I do not think so. I think IR will continue to report to the CFO or CEO—so having the IRO on the leadership team as well, next to the CEO or CFO, would be doubling structures unnecessarily.
>
> However, if the question is, "Will IR be participating increasingly in boardroom meetings at the top level?" the answer is: "Definitely, yes."
>
> *Constantin Fest*
> SVP/Head of IR
> GSK

The likeliest development for IR going forward, therefore, is that this will increasingly be its role—a growing boardroom presence, but still reporting into the CFO.

"CHIEF REPUTATION OFFICER"?

Investor relations has always operated at the intersection of various disciplines, influencing them but never quite *of* them: Communications, legal, strategy, sustainability, and more. At one level, it speaks to IR's unique strengths: A multi-skilled executive counsel, able to take a view across overlapping functional areas and apply that combined intelligence to the needs of capital markets.

But it also puts IR in a weak position whenever the corporate tectonic plates shift and fiefdoms are built to address emerging concerns. Having no single expertise in these areas, IR risks being squeezed out by the creation of new standing departments—and losing power in the process.

I suffer from different parts of the company interacting with different stakeholders and telling different stories. Message consistency is so critical that IR will have to become more integrated into corporate affairs. It may even end up taking over the function entirely (depending on the company size). I can certainly foresee it reporting directly to the CEO, in charge of not only the relationship with investors and sell-side but also all internal and external communications, ESG, etc.

Juan Gaitan
Director of Investor Relations
CELLNEX TELECOM

Today, the clearest example is IR's investment of energy in ESG/ sustainability, even as large-cap companies are increasingly creating specialized functions to own the issue. Then there is the eternally vexed issue of corporate affairs.

In most FTSE 100 companies, the silos still exist between IR and corporate affairs, and I understand why: investor relations has some very specific technical requirements, and the competencies you need to engage with the capital markets are different for sure, and if you haven't had exposure to them, it's difficult to understand how it all works. So it's rare to find someone who has experience in both IR and broader corporate communications.

But at Ocado, it would seem perverse to have IR and corporate affairs operating in separate silos. If you don't get the conversation right with the capital markets, all the other conversations are out of alignment. The IR piece of communications is like the cornerstone of a cathedral—you take it out, and the whole building falls in.

David Shriver
Former Chief Reputation Officer -
OCADO

I think it will become necessary for IR and other comms functions to merge in a more strategic manner. The audience consuming the news media, after all, is often part of IR's larger stakeholder group, so the company's messaging need to be convincingly aligned. The digital world has a huge role to play here.

Lorna Davie
President
IR CLUB SWITZERLAND
& Former Director, Investor Relations
CREDIT SUISSE/UBS

CASE STUDY: INFORMA

Today, CEOs of public companies have no option but to have a close working relationship with their IRO: They need to sign off on an ESG policy that will be scrutinized by analysts as a measure of the company's commercial viability. Their every market-sensitive utterance must coherently weave together the company's commercial plans and its strategy for reputational growth.

It has not only led to a new working alliance between IROs and CEOs—the two now commonly spending weeks together ahead of major investor events, shaping that narrative into an agreed, market-acceptable portrait of the company's public positioning. In an emerging number of cases, it has led to the IRO being moved onto the ExCo and given wholesale responsibility for all communications to be able to coordinate the reputational narrative—since it's in IR that the CEO has seen that narrative be fostered and grown.

One such example is the UK's FTSE50 company Informa.

"Our incoming CEO viewed communications strategically," says Richard Menzies Gow, director of investor relations, corporate communications and brand. "He's always felt, in particular, that the message should be consistent across investors and colleagues, especially around sustainability; a golden thread to everything in terms of the narrative.

"So when we went through a whole strategy review and created an executive management team, it was at that point he said to me, as IR director: 'Right, you're going to just take control of the whole comms piece—as well as sustainability and IR—and bring it all together, make it all make sense.' And that was that.

"So we've now arrived at that future: I'm 'director of investor relations, corporate communications & brand', and I have a sustainability team, a comms team and an IR team, but they're interconnected and naturally that means there's consistency in what we're saying and how we're saying it."

For as long as IR has been in existence, there have been calls for it to be brought into closer alignment with other communications teams—even into the same reporting line. After all, both IR and the "comms collective" that typically sits under corporate affairs (i.e., media relations, PR, internal communications, government relations and public affairs) are trafficking in the company story—in building it, protecting it, and deploying it. How successful can that endeavor be if the two groups aren't working in lock step?

For many years, both IR and communications have resisted formal convergence—different audiences, we say. Different skills. Different knowledge base. Fundamentally different approaches. A different attitude to facts.

But the evidence is that this argument is running out of road—and fast.

First, because the audiences and narrative are increasingly the same: Asset managers are as much target audiences for the company's PR and media relations as for its IR, with investors weighing the company's brand and public reputation as much as its financial strategy. Employees are customers, who are also retail investors, who are also today's "media," with public voices on Twitter/X, TikTok and Instagram. Anti-corporate activists, the ambit of PR, increasingly target firms' supply chains and cost bases, or block their expansion and investment plans. Investor activism, meanwhile, increasingly leverages the company's wider, intangible communications positioning (notably, its sustainability profile and brand strength).

Truly, it has never been more essential for there to be one company communications position, consistent across all audiences.

Second, because in increasing numbers of corporations in the last few years, these factors have led to the incorporation of vast, all-encompassing, executive-level corporate affairs functions. IR may have enjoyed growing responsibilities and influence in recent years. But so has corporate affairs. In many large- and medium-cap companies, fueled by the C-Suite's sudden eagerness for a "hub" of reputational oversight in the room, an executive corporate affairs function is now absorbing not just traditional internal and external

> I continue to believe that IR should be part of the finance function, while maintaining its strong, direct links with the CEO, company secretary and chair of the Board. As long as the IRO has the right stakeholder-management capabilities, it is perhaps the most advantageous position—to be closely intertwined with finance, but with strong links of independent influence.
>
> *Matthew Johnson*
> Group Communications Director,
> IR & CEO Office,
> VODAFONE

communications, but public and government affairs, brand and marketing, ESG and sustainability, even strategy. In some cases, we have seen them absorb IR as well.

This seems to be a generational shift in ExCo belief systems: Reputation is too diffuse and complex today—and too easy to fracture—for it to be managed by a decentralized federation of departments anymore. It needs executive oversight from a single point of influence.

So as both IR and corporate affairs have expanded, they are also encroaching on each other's territory more than ever before. And with greater influence, and greater potential power, the turf wars of such overlaps could turn nuclear. At Broome Yasar, it is very noticeable how similar our discussions with senior corporate affairs leaders and senior IROs are today—almost identical remits; same sense of reputational guardianship; same stated need to be across both tangibles and intangibles; and, most of all, the stated need by both parties for them to "own" ESG/sustainability in order to be effective.

I see the synergy between IR and other comms functions evolving as companies seek to communicate a more integrated message to stakeholders. I also believe IR will become more integrated into corporate affairs, as companies recognize the importance of aligned messaging. I don't think IR will take over corporate affairs, but I do see it as a natural training ground for future heads of corporate affairs.

Maximilian Zimmermann Canovas
President and Cofounder of INARI and Investor Relations and Sustainability Director at Grupo Hotelero Santa Fe

---

That all appears to be leading us towards an almighty battle and a few possible, inevitable conclusions for IR. Either this mushrooming corporate affairs function will absorb (in whole or in part) investor relations. Or it will at least gain much more influence over it.

The other alternative, for an investor relations profession also on the rise, is that IR perhaps becomes the breeding ground for a new era of corporate affairs leaders. We have seen this too, in companies like Experian (see case study), where the IRO's individual talents, and their working-life proximity to the CEO/CFO, made them the "obvious" guardian of the company narrative—and therefore the "natural" choice as the next head of corporate affairs.

But whatever the outcome, it is clear that the importance of reputation management to the ExCo, and the importance of "owning" ESG/sustainability to the future of both corporate

---

ESG will become more of a given in the IR space as we move forward. IR professionals will have to be very well-versed in ESG requirements, both current and upcoming, to ensure their company is prepared to fulfil future capital-market expectations. IR must play a leading role, becoming the tip of the spear when it comes to recognizing external change and ensuring internal preparedness.

Sustainability reporting will become more and more integrated; ESG metrics will become more and more like "traditional" performance metrics. All of which means that corporations (and IR) will have to get used to reporting them, giving guidance on them and tracking their own progress on them in order to communicate clearly where they stand.

Constantin Fest
SVP/Head of IR
GSK

---

affairs and IR, means that somewhere, somehow, some kind of convergence is on the horizon. IROs therefore need to beware the growing size and influence of corporate affairs: If the threat is taken too lightly—if it is seen as just another bit of diplomacy to manage in a decades-long tale of push/pull over respective spheres of influence—IR may find itself the victim of first mover's advantage.

CASE STUDY: EXPERIAN

In recent years, a series of catalysts in common—heightened boardroom sensitivity about reputation; increased importance of sustainability; and increased professionalization—have significantly blurred the lines between the remits of IR and corporate affairs. Indeed, the overarching briefs are now almost identical in large organizations: Define, shape and safeguard the reputational narrative.

It's important to remember: CEOs are agnostic about who pulls which lever to achieve that outcome, and they increasingly see the needs of investors, consumers and employees as an integrated whole. They just want the fragile corporate reputation stage-managed by a central executive function. But by increasing the access and influence of both IR and corporate affairs in recent years, they have set the two on a collision course for the same role.

"Consistency matters more than ever before for companies, because we're all being held responsible for a much wider sphere of activity," explains Experian's Nadia Ridout-Jamieson in *From Band Leader to Master Conductor*, our report detailing the recent explosive growth of an executive-level corporate affairs profession. Broome Yasar helped appoint Ridout-Jamieson as head of investor relations at the FTSE30 company just a few years ago—but today she leads a combined function as its chief communications officer.

"If you think about it from a CEO's point of view, they're responsible for everything in the company. It doesn't matter whether it's strategy or risk or operations or brand—or how we communicate with investors or how we communicate with employees. So you're trying to achieve a single voice for the company through everything, and bringing IR and communications together just helps with that consistency."

IR's remit and where it sits will be different for different firms—depending on the individual IRO and the wider company culture. (Personally, for instance, I'm less interested in corporate affairs but enjoy thinking about the big picture in the long-term, so I lean more towards strategy.) But the IR function needs to be collaborative to be successful, so you must build great relationships regardless—not only with comms, but with finance, legal, function heads, and so on.

Ashish Kohli
VP Investor Relations
GENERAL MOTORS

"ESG IRO"?

In the last few years, consumers have begun to take a brand's purpose deadly seriously. In response, so have shareholders: In today's hair-trigger, media-drenched world, investors clearly see brand equity as the commercial strategy in many ways; solid public reputation as a core reason for investing in a firm. Not least because regulators and their customers expect ethics too.

And this is not just a passing vogue, nor is it a tributary concern. In many jurisdictions, it's now law, with a structured ESG strategy a pre-requisite for being allowed to attract institutional investment.

By natural extension, therefore, after decades of giving lip service to "CSR" and its various offshoots, Boards really do now care about the company's sustainability profile. Just look at the US, where the proportion of S&P 500 firms reporting on ESG performance grew from less than 20% a decade ago to 90% now.[6]

Investor relations has therefore responded to that call with gusto in recent years. Our interviewees were almost universally adamant that ESG and sustainability had become as important to IR as oxygen is to breathing—that the integration of ESG into the company narrative has become the norm, and that IR should be leading the discussion on how the sustainability narrative is realized, and coordinate the internal processes

---

[6] Governance & Accountability Institute, Inc., Annual 2020 Flash Report https://www.ga-institute.com/ga-research-collection/sustainability-reporting-trends/2020-sp-500-flash-report/

to ensure progress is planned, measured and communicated internally and externally.

"ESG is rising in importance for the investment community," explained Eva Chan, Chair of the Hong Kong IR Association, for example. "Questions on ESG and the company's ESG rating actively affect the firm's valuation, so IROs have no choice but to equip themselves with deep knowledge of ESG. And since ESG needs to deal with different stakeholders, IROs are increasingly required to take part in many different types of stakeholder engagements. It's why, driven by the ESG dynamic, I see the role of investor relations expanding into a broader 'stakeholder relations' role over the coming years."

BUT IS ESG REALLY A PART OF IR'S *FUTURE*—OR JUST A VERY IMPORTANT PART OF ITS PRESENT?

The question is ... where will the cards on this issue fall as we move forward through the decade?

> ESG measures, I expect, will become an increasingly important aspect of investment evaluation: Our youth are demanding it and traditional portfolio managers globally are too. In the not-too-distant future, ESG measures may become equally as important as financial measures. Certainly, they are part of the overall equation, and I don't believe there'll be a way to get around it as a public company in the future.
>
> *Laura Kiernan*
> **Senior Vice President**
> **RIVEL, INC**

First because many different functions in a typical multinational feel ownership over parts of the ESG/sustainability remit (not least corporate affairs, legal and strategy), which means IR could be heading for bitter turf wars, if it isn't in the thick of those battles already.

Second, because many organizations now have standing ESG/sustainability departments, or are busy building them—so attempts to "own" the issue may prove futile (indeed, self-

My personal view is that IROs worldwide have been far too quick to jump on the ESG bandwagon. This is potentially a dangerous mistake.

On the institutional side, investors have arguably been too quick to market funds as 'sustainable'—often by doing no more than changing the fund's name. (Many will remember a similar rebranding rush during the internet bubble.) Recent moves to counteract greenwashing are very welcome but we may well find, when the ESG bubble deflates, that the actual size of the sustainable investing universe is significantly smaller than we all thought.

On the corporate side, IROs would do well to remember who their core constituency is—investors! The idea of stakeholder capitalism has been unhelpful in this respect, with the implication that companies are equally obligated to other constituencies. That's not to say customers, employees and suppliers are unimportant. They're just not the owners of the company and not the primary concern of an IRO.

One final thought: It has been easy in economically good times for companies to wax lyrical about the importance of other 'stakeholders'; in economically difficult times, when difficult decisions will need to be taken by many companies, we may see a return to old-fashioned shareholder capitalism.

Matthew O'Keeffe
Managing Director
FTI CONSULTING

defeating if IR has gambled all its influence on doing so). Not least because, third, several firms today fill their ESG need with external agency support.

"Many IROs are heavily involved in ESG communication," said Clara Melia, Founder and CEO of Equitory. "But my expectation is that more companies will hire internal specialist teams around ESG and sustainability matters in the next two to three years. It will also be interesting to watch how AI technology can support in this area, particularly around screening companies' disclosures for ratings agencies—so it may be that much of what IR is involved in today around ESG ends up being automated."

Our interviewees were therefore conflicted on the issue. All were clear that ESG and sustainability had become central to the IR role as it is performed today. All were clear that it had become a central spine of the equity story being presented to the investment world. But several industry observers felt it was an issue that, ultimately, would fade from view for IR professionals; just one more part of the overall brand mix of "intangibles" to be factored into the company narrative.

But as I had highlighted before, it's all too soon to see what the fundamental impact on this important area is likely with the approach on Trumpism on these critical arenas.

I think **ESG** is a buzzword, and it will likely lose some luster moving forward and be replaced more and more by 'being socially responsible'.

Ashish Kohli
VP Investor Relations
GENERAL MOTORS

The Evolution of IR Priorities

IROs were asked: How important do you expect the following issues to be in the coming year?
Responses ranked issues by priority:

2013	2019	2023
1. Keeping on top of regulatory changes	1. ESG Communications	1. Targeting Right Investors
2. Targeting Right Investors	2. Targeting Right Investors	2. Managing Guidance & Consensus
3. Raising importance of IR at Board level	3. Managing Guidance & Consensus	3. ESG Communications
4. Managing Disclosure requirements	4. Measuring the success of IR activities	4. Measuring the success of IR activities
5. Obtaining good shareholder Identification	5. Corporate access & research	5. Raising importance of IR at Board level
6. Corporate Governance and voting	6. Raising importance of IR at Board level	6. The role / use of AI in IR
7. Managing Guidance & Consensus	7. Adapting to post-MiFID II environment	7. Activism
8. Changes in Integrated Reporting	8. Corporate Governance and voting	8. Retail investors

Data from Annual IR Society Membership Survey over 10 years from 2013 to 2023.
IR Soc determined 'issues' on a year-by-year basis.

Analysis by QuantiFire of a decade of annual IR Society (UK) Membership Survey results, reveals ESG rising up the priority list by the late 2010s ... then tailing away again in the most recent survey

The Importance of ESG in Investment Decision Making

ESG clearly impacts investment decisions (but there are signs that its importance may be plateauing)

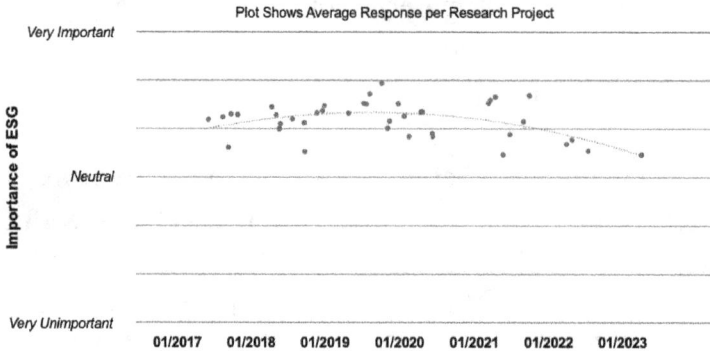

Analysis shows results of 40 research projects, each of which asked 'How important is ESG in your decision making process'. Over 4,000 answers to this question were obtained from investors.

That is borne out by QuantiFire's analysis of 4,000 investor survey responses over 2017-2023: ESG currently rates its lowest importance quotient score with investors over that period, and the trend (since a 2019/20 peak) appears on a downward trend

"ROBO IRO"?

The era's great disruptor—artificial intelligence (AI)—is frittering nerves in almost every corporate function. Friend or foe? The end of the profession, or its liberation?

It is hard to dismiss the potential impact AI might have on IR when a series of technological advancements in recent years have already altered so much of the role, from its basic channel ecosystem (e.g., the vastly increased use of social media and virtual meetings) to research (through ever more elaborate and granular data analytics), to investment strategies (most notably the boom in passive investing/indexing), to the profile of the typical shareholder (by simplifying retail investment, especially for millennials and Gen Z, in the smartphone and app era).

With the addition of AI to that heady brew, is IR going to become a deeply technological role in the near future? Or—perhaps—a much less one?

The significant advances in technology and increasing use of generative AI, large language models and machine learning are heralding a new dawn in IR. We must adapt to this rapidly changing environment—for example, by becoming increasingly competent as data scientists and prompt engineers—to guide senior management and Boards through this new landscape, identifying challenges and opportunities in applying this technology to communications and strategy. However, these changes will not replace our ability as humans to build meaningful relationships predicated on trust—a key tenet of good investor relations.

Nick Stone
SVP, Head of Investor Relations
Fresenius

MANY POSSIBLE AI-ENABLED FUTURES

Here is one scenario, for example: A highly tech-savvy IRO in an AI-supported world would have almost limitless ability to map existing and potential shareholders to investment requirements and opportunities, and could auto-devise the optimal tactics for reaching them, supporting them and communicating the exact information they required. The IR role would become a daily re-engineering of the code, finding ever more ingenious ways of unearthing investors with the right information, transforming the IRO hiring profile into one of a highly skilled IT technician, with perhaps some supporting communications and finance expertise in their skillset.

An AI-liberated IR function, on the other hand, would use external technology experts to build algorithmic models to let the tech do all of that hard work automatically—freeing up the IRO themselves to focus on strategy, and on the one-to-one relationships that will surely never stop being fundamental requirements of the role.

> I don't think we should be afraid of AI actually. I think that, especially when you have a very small team, which I do now—there's just two of us—it's an addition to the team. I spend so much time doing the first draft, or trying to figure something out. But you can just ask the machine, and then put your strategic touch to it. So I don't think we should [feel] threatened. And there is one thing the machine cannot replace: the relations part of investor relations.
>
> *Isabelle Adjahi*
> **Vice President, Communications**
> **CDPQ**

For now, we are in that unstable moment of being directly in the eye of the hurricane—living at the very moment of revolutionary change, when it is still unclear how the world will emerge when the storm has passed. Specifically, we cannot yet confidently predict the profile of a typical IRO in an AI-enabled world, or the company's expectations of the IR function a decade from now when AI is an established part of all our working lives.

What seems clear is that AI will undoubtedly play an increasing role in fulfilling some of the more routine aspects of the daily role—the day cannot be far away when much of the work around reporting will be driven by AI, or even

---

What I say is, no, AI is not going to replace you, but someone who can use AI better than you might.

Erik Carlson
COO and CFO
NOTIFIED

Freeing up IR from the more mundane processing, filtering and sorting tasks of the IR toolkit means more possibilities for value-added strategic thinking, planning and execution alongside management and the Board.

While not quite "robo-IRO," it is easier to envisage a more productive day in the life of IR coming over the horizon. This will need to happen as other related tasks, like ESG and sustainability reporting, become part and parcel of the role of IR. Clever use of technology can free up the busy IRO for a more strategic role. This, in turn, will enable the best IROs to prove themselves as trusted advisers to management and the Board.

John Gollifer
Former General Manager
THE MIDDLE EAST IR ASSOCIATION (MEIRA)

---

fully automated; investor targeting too. One interviewee pointed out to us that this could then drive a case for some of IR's current role being more absorbed into other parts of the finance function. "In that world," she said, "more of the emphasis for IR will be on the strategy, the competitive positioning of the company and its valuation—which, to my mind, is the most interesting part of IR today."

But it seems clear that many of the more nuanced aspects of the job—and the development of the all-important relationships with stakeholders—will always still require the skills of an experienced and trusted IRO. The color analysis of that world, one-to-one, with stakeholders, is something AI cannot do, and it doesn't look like it will ever be able to—at least not for now.

At our core in IR, we take endless amounts of data and distill it into an insightful and engaging narrative. With the increasing influx of AI, machine learning and social media, what becomes even more important are the parts played by human interaction and the emotive side of investor engagement.

So I see the daily IR role evolving in two ways. Firstly, we need to have real-time access to enhanced data to be effective (including macroeconomic and industry data, information on daily stock purchasing, internal performance, competitors, etc.). Secondly, we need to re-gear our skillset to focus more on the "Relations" part of our job title: Broad, deep and strong relationships within the organization and throughout the investment community are becomingly increasingly important, not less, with the ever growing oceans of data.

Matthew Johnson
Group Communications Director,
IR & CEO Office,
VODAFONE

The Transformative Impact Of Artificial Intelligence On Investor Relations: A Blessing Or A Curse?

I thought it important to gauge the views of Extel on the question, other than macroeconomic issues, of how our industry needs to adapt to the inevitable power of AI. Here Amani Korayeim shares her thoughts on this likely future.

In recent times, the convergence of artificial intelligence (AI) and digitization within the realm of Investor Relations (IR) has garnered significant attention, almost overshadowing discussions on regulatory compliance and environmental, social, and governance (ESG) considerations. This trend is evident in the numerous IR conferences and discussions held by leading IR teams worldwide.

IMPORTANCE OF THE TOPIC

More than a buzzword or a boardroom fad, understanding the implications of AI in IR is crucial due to the potential advantages it offers, alongside the inherent risks involved. These advantages include enhanced time management, strategic resource allocation, accelerated product development, and more efficient interaction with market participants, all of which contribute to overall success in IR. While the advantages of AI integration are significant, the counterarguments are multifaceted and necessitate thorough deliberation. These encompass, among others, the risk of data breaches, compromising data privacy and security, the potential for inaccurate or biased decision making and outcomes stemming from the use of non-representative data, and the possibility of a lack of transparency in data modelling processes.

IR has continually faced pressures to adapt and deliver, making it a perpetual challenge for the function. It is undergoing rapid evolution which underscores the importance of emphasizing agility, focus, and adopting a Know Your Customer (KYC) approach to its structures and working processes. Succeeding in IR necessitates the capacity to adjust to constantly fluctuating market dynamics, regulatory changes, and the growing need for improved, expedited, and more efficient information and communication.

The most effective IR teams prioritize maintaining robust relationships with their stakeholders, comprehensively understanding their requirements, and striving to align with and mirror their processes.

To have a measured discussion on the role of AI in IR, it's important to consider how stakeholders are utilizing smart technology tools to access data, construct and rebalance portfolios, and make informed investment decisions.

In the past, prominent investors heavily relied on their finely tuned intuition. However, nowadays, they frequently complement or even supplant this reliance with advanced analytics and third-party data to craft intricate financial and business models. The transition represents a notable obstacle for investor relations departments.

The task of maintaining precise and uniform corporate data across various platforms is already a formidable undertaking for IR teams. This challenge is exacerbated by the expanding volume of data, along with the swift technological progress that empowers investors to promptly make well-informed choices. Consequently, IR teams must remain vigilant to monitor, interact with, and address market sentiments effectively.

Screening sentiment data is not only useful for identifying negative market reactions, but it also produces valuable insights on the effectiveness of IR communication and their content delivery strategy.

AI has been identified as a game-changing technology that is transforming various sectors. Businesses and teams are currently exploring AI tools in three broad categories:

1. Technological tools that improve the efficiency of stakeholder interactions.
2. Business enablers that enhance processes, methods, and systems.
3. The ability to facilitate the intersection of different technologies for a quicker and more solution-focused approach.

Investors frequently rely on natural language processing tools to analyze historical and current data. These tools enable investors to sift through various sources of information, such as call transcripts, company websites, and social media platforms to identify trends, monitor market sentiment, track portfolio performance, and obtain real-time insights. By leveraging these tools, investors can make informed investment decisions and better assess portfolio risks.

When reviewing Extel's annual independent Corporate Insights research ©2023/24, which entails surveying c.2,000 IR

Professionals across Europe, Asia, Emerging EMEA, Japan, US, and Latin America, it is evident that AI and digitized applications are already impacting some areas of their activities. These activities are almost consistent across all six regional markets and primarily consist of administrative or tactical components requiring increased levels of automation, independent of establishing or nurturing human-led stakeholder relationships.

As we examine the list of activities by region, we observe that the integration of advanced technology may vary depending on factors such as market maturity, IR professionalization, linguistic challenges, sector, or company size.

1. Communication and Press Releases
2. Events Organization
3. Virtual vs Physical Engagement

North America	Europe	Asia
1. Communication & press releases	1. Virtual & physical engagement	1. Communication and press releases
2. Virtual & physical engagement	2. Events (AGM, virtual site visits & investor events)	2. Events (AGM, virtual site visits & investor events)
3. Events (AGM, virtual site visits & investor events)	3. Communication and press releases	3. Virtual and physical engagement
4. Targeting	4. Shareholder ID	4. Contact engagement platform
5. Contact & engagement platform	5. Targeting	5. Executive management engagement
South America	**Africa**	**SE Asia**
1. Communication & press releases	1. Virtual & physical engagement	1. Communication and press releases
2. Events (AGM, virtual site visits & investor events)	2. Events (AGM, virtual site visits & investor events)	2. Virtual and physical engagement
3. Virtual & physical engagement	3. Communication and press releases	3. Events (AGM, virtual site visits & investor events)
4. Website interaction tools	4. Shareholder ID	4. Contact engagement platform
5. Executive management engagement	5. Targeting	5. Translation tools

Top IR activities impacted most by generative AI and digitization application by region.

© Extel Research & Rankings, Global
Executive Team Surveys, 2023

COMMUNICATION AND PRESS RELEASES

Generating marketing communication materials, such as quarterly reports, proxy statements, press releases, summary reports and FAQs for stakeholders, is a time-consuming process that typically requires several staff members. However, with the implementation of generative AI, these tasks can now be accomplished in a fraction of the time.

Despite the efficiency and cost-effectiveness provided by AI tools, it remains imperative to conduct human oversight and thorough examination of publicly available company data. This practice ensures not only accuracy but also adherence to securities and regulatory standards. Utilizing generative AI for crafting communications aimed at shareholders and investors entails inherent risks. There is a heightened probability of inaccuracies or notable omissions, potentially leading to the inadvertent dissemination of misleading information. Moreover, intentionally censoring words or phrases by AI to sidestep raising concerns could result in a flattened or manipulated message, casting doubt on the veracity and credibility of the content and, consequently, on the reliability of the company and its leadership.

EVENTS ORGANIZATION

Exceptional IR teams, beyond conducting Annual General Meetings (AGMs), uphold consistent engagement with stakeholders via tailored events centered on growth opportunities, product advancements, business updates, and corporate access. These engagements are frequently facilitated through smaller, more personalized investor gatherings like fireside chats or on-site visits, aiming to bolster transparency and cultivate robust relationships with stakeholders.

Companies are consistently striving to enhance the value they offer to their investors in exchange for their time. Great IR teams, in partnership with internal or outsourced event teams, are determined to provide more immersive and participatory experiences that reinforce the equity narrative and foster confidence in the company's vision and leadership.

AI can enhance aspects of event planning, including venue selection, concept development and marketing. Moreover, it can lead to a more customized experience for attendees, catering to their individual interests and preferences. However, it's crucial to ensure that while adopting a personalized approach, equal access and disclosure to information is maintained, and individual privacy and data are protected at all times.

If companies have accumulated information on attendees through prior engagements and events, AI can utilize this data to tailor a more personalized event experience. By utilizing Natural Language Processing (NLP), companies can analyze words, themes, and questions to help shape the content for specific workshops that relate to the respective audience. Virtual and augmented reality can play a vital role in showcasing present and future facilities and plans, especially if challenging to access or at concept.

In certain markets, where linguistic barriers can impede effective and consistent communication and dissemination of messaging, countries such as Japan have embraced AI tools that enable instantaneous and synchronized translation. This technology has become a staple at events and other key investment engagements.

VIRTUAL VS PHYSICAL ENGAGEMENT

Undeniably, the pandemic has accelerated the integration of technology, especially in communication. Presently, both external and internal communication platforms play a pivotal role in our daily work activities. Virtual meetings have significantly improved the capacity for IR to interact with a vast number of investors across various geographical areas, facilitating more effective and diversified investor outreach efforts within a typical workday.

In the interest of streamlining interactions and optimizing the time of C-suite executives, some leaders are contemplating utilizing avatars as proxies to conduct earnings calls and other investor communications. This approach aims to mitigate the scrutiny of speech patterns. While this anodyne approach might sound a safe option, there are associated risks. It may also contradict the current trend of investors and analysts seeking in-person, authentic interactions. The pandemic had resulted in a dearth of physical meetings, but we are now enjoying a resurgence in demand for them. The ability to understand nonverbal signals, like body language, strong handshakes, casual pre-meeting conversations, and eye contact, can greatly influence how a meeting is perceived. Nonverbal cues, therefore, play a crucial role in shaping investors' intuitive judgment, assisting them in extracting valuable insights and enhancing their decision-making processes.

In an effort to refine their decision-making processes, investors are progressively turning to tools that scrutinize speech patterns, tone, and behavioral cues exhibited by executive management teams during pivotal events like earnings calls and corporate presentations. Within this context, IR assumes a central role in orchestrating engaging and impactful interactions. Through meticulous scripting, choreography, and rigorous rehearsal of these market-facing activities, IR ensures that the Executive Management teams deliver presentations that resonate with their audience. Given the potential challenges posed by probing inquiries from investment professionals during Q&A sessions, even with the aid of analytical tools, thorough preparation becomes paramount. Ultimately, IR bears the responsibility of bolstering management's credibility and fostering a perception of trustworthiness as a dependable source of company information.

CONCLUSION

While AI technology offers significant potential to streamline processes and reduce the time and resources dedicated to manual tasks, it's imperative to emphasize that AI should be used responsibly and with caution and should not replace humans. Rather, it should be leveraged as a tool to enhance human effectiveness and productivity, enabling individuals to focus on more strategic aspects of their work.

It's essential to recognize the potential dangers of generative AI in creating biased financial models. Utilizing non-diverse or statistically unrepresentative datasets can perpetuate existing inequalities, thus highlighting the need for caution. Such distinct set of risks call for strict regulations. The deployment of AI should be sustainable and constructive, prioritizing positive outcomes.

Regulatory and compliance reviews are underway in multiple markets to prevent potential misuse and abuse, especially in financial and capital markets. The complexity of generative models and deep learning technology may result in a lack of transparency, posing a potential threat to market stability.

The Securities and Exchange Commission (SEC), for example, has formed a task force to focus on AI and has designated it as a priority. Similarly, the EU is developing a regulatory framework to manage the use of AI, classifying risks into high and minimal risk categories.

The buzz surrounding ESG over recent years and the need to comply with associated regulations has led to several instances of green washing, which is reminiscent of some of the behavior we can witness now around the AI narrative, referred to by SEC chair, Gary Gensler, as "herd behavior." Similarly, the adoption of AI may lead to comparable outcomes in the short-term. According to Adriano Koshiyama, the co-founder and co-CEO of Holistic AI, 2023 was "the year of AI awareness," and he cautions that the next few years may witness "lawsuits, fines, and big cases" that will serve as watershed events in the AI conversation and help identify risks and threats to shape regulatory guidelines and principles.

IR teams are consistently under pressure to outperform competitors and fulfill stakeholder demands. The deployment of streamlined processes and strategic resource distribution becomes imperative in this competitive landscape. While a few organizations have begun incorporating AI into their practices, a considerable number of firms adopt a more prudent "wait and see" approach, attentively monitoring advancements in product development and innovation.

The integration of AI into IR requires a responsible approach that emphasizes transparency, ethics, and regulatory compliance. By prioritizing these factors, decision-making and work processes can be improved by augmenting human expertise rather than replacing it. Such an approach will maximize benefits for both stakeholders and the organization.

Amani Korayeim
Director Corporate Product & Partnerships
Europe/EMEA, Extel

extel

"VIRTUAL IRO"?

The clearest disagreement among our interviewees about IR's technology-enabled future concerned perhaps its most prosaic elements: The increasing use of social media for outreach, and the post-Covid shift to online investor meetings.

The "virtual IRO" role that has emerged certainly has its fans—but also significant detractors.

> Covid has fundamentally changed many practical elements in IR here in Hong Kong. Virtual meetings, rather than physical, became the new normal, and the reopening of the border with China hasn't changed things back entirely. Having said that, face-to-face meetings with investors are still required as part of the package, since trust and relationships are built more easily through physical touchpoints—but the travel budget to allow for that is now proving difficult to get back in the same way as before.
>
> *Eva Chan*
> Chair
> **HONG KONG IR ASSOCIATION**

ARE ONLINE MEETINGS HERE TO STAY?

Although they had been around for some time in various formats, virtual investor meetings had never truly gained the traction and appeal of in-person shareholder forums—until a global pandemic came along and changed everything entirely overnight. Suddenly, none of us had a choice anymore.

But those years have normalized online engagement, and many of our IROs and industry experts felt that virtual meetings were now an established, inevitable vision of IR's future. Indeed, some noted it had almost become an expectation among investor audiences. In a globalized world of international shareholders, and with many of them small retail investors lacking the budget to travel (indeed, in economically straitened times, with even larger shareholders perhaps finding their travel allowance less forgiving than in previous years), these interviewees felt that it just made sense to foreground virtual investor meetings. Apart from anything else, which of us isn't now perfectly acclimated to MS Teams and Zoom meetings—in all business contexts— as a perfectly acceptable analogue for meeting in person? It has gone from curiosity to common to absolutely normal in a few short years.

Others, however, pointed to the strong counter evidence: In particular declining attendance at virtual investor meetings— and declining engagement among those who do attend. These IR leaders and experts sensed a growing desire for a return to the world of face-to-face engagement; of real, human interaction; of the unique qualities that meeting in person

---

Covid's legacy will be in forcing IR to live with a hybrid approach. Some investors are heartily sick of virtual meetings now and I believe there will be rewards for those companies prepared to venture out and meet investors in person once again. Other investors, however, are quite content to work remotely and it must be said that, at FTI, we observe an occasionally lackadaisical approach to the physical events we organize. It is not easy to explain this; hybrid working seems to have encouraged a non-committal approach to in-person meetings. The hybrid approach looks set to stay, for now, but few of the companies I deal with find it entirely satisfactory.

Matthew O'Keeffe
Managing Director
FTI CONSULTING

---

brings—the ability to shake hands; to see eye-to-eye; to have perhaps a quiet conversation in the margins with someone one-to one, then draw others in as required; and to judge the mood of the room utilizing all of the non-verbal cues that are as strong a part of the communication receptors in our human brains as our verbal language receptors.

It's a compelling argument, albeit it comes with the danger of mis-identifying your own desire for someone else's. (See also: The common corporate commentary, post-Covid, of those sensing a real desire out there among people to return to the office which, we would observe, was a "desire" mostly "sensed" and articulated by managers and executives, not front-line employees.) Certainly, for IR, personal engagement is fundamental to building effective relationships with buyers—but is it considered *as* fundamental among investors to travel to meet with IR departments face to face? The most likely answer would surely be that it depends on the investor—that different people will have wildly different preferences on this, and therefore that, to reach all of its audiences, IR will now have to accommodate a hybrid model into the future.

Virtual meetings have become globally accepted and have opened new portals for meeting with investors. I believe IROs and investors alike will take advantage of "access anytime, anywhere" and it will enable more pinpoint targeting of audiences and messaging. I also believe social media will become standard as one of the ways companies distribute their messages and communicate with investors and analysts.

Laura Kiernan
Senior Vice President
RIVEL, INC

In this, perhaps IR has been a victim of its own success: It was able to deliver successfully during Covid-19, despite its inability to arrange large international gatherings. Why then, would it need anything different now?

IS IR'S FUTURE FULL OF SOCIAL MEDIA?

Likewise, there were polarized views among our interviewees on the value of social media as a key part of IR's future.

There were certainly evangelists—people who felt not only that social media was an increasingly essential communication tool in IR, but one that IR had been too slow to capitalize upon and whose potential many still hadn't even nearly realized. The business model of all of the social-media giants, after all, is in their exquisite targeting—something other communications professions have eagerly seized upon. (Today, for example, it would be extremely unusual in public relations, marketing and advertising to run a campaign that did not have a very strong paid social-media component—because the hard work of audience segmentation and targeting is already done. This is what social

---

LinkedIn is an increasingly important communication channel for companies and should be considered part of the IR strategy. With any social media strategy, companies should have strong controls in place to minimize the disclosure risk. LinkedIn is also a powerful tool for expanding an individual's network amongst other IROs and market participants, and to develop their personal brand to support their career progression.

Clara Melia
Founder and CEO
EQUITORY

media platforms sell: The ability to find the person you want better than you can yourselves, down to the most detailed parameters.)

But at the other end of the axis, we also had outright skeptics, who felt that social media had proven to be a complete bust as a means of interacting with investors; that it was certainly not taken seriously by institutional investors as a business communication tool when discussing multi-million-dollar shareholdings; and that it was perhaps an area of investor communications most ripe for handing over to large-language-model AI programs to use for the most prosaic of communication tasks. For anything that required genuine engagement, they felt, social media was not the answer.

Social Media Importance

How Important Do You Believe Social Media Is As A Means of Communication With the Buy Side:

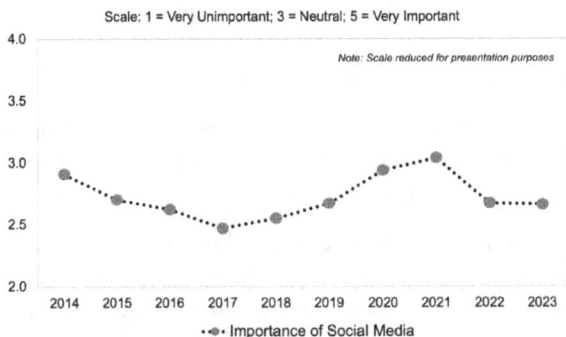

Scale: 1 = Very Unimportant; 3 = Neutral; 5 = Very Important

Note: Scale reduced for presentation purposes

• Importance of Social Media

Results are based on responses from corporate IR Society Members, provided as part of an Annual Membership Survey

QuantiFire's annual survey of the UK IR Society's membership (n= ~122 annually), shows UK IROs cooling on social media as an investor communication tool

In most organizations, perhaps, what we learn is that social media communications will have to be a part of an increasingly very complex channel mix to capture those for whom it works—but the "fully virtual IRO" is not a proposition that looks likely any time soon.

"ROI IRO"?

To level up the profession, we may also need to think differently about what IR is, and how it can thereby deliver stronger return on investment (ROI). Or how we can repackage and re-sell what IR already does, to showcase its benefits more effectively. Our interviewees brought forward numerous ideas for how IR can deliver and demonstrate more added value to the business.

From taking the lead on peer benchmarking, to building analyst models, to collaborating with stock exchanges to officially rank investor communications, our interviewees were keen to show how IR's unrivalled positioning, skillset and

---

Imagine if your company received an annual rating on how effectively it communicated with investors. For listed companies in Bucharest, that has been the reality for the past five years.

Every year, the Romanian Investor Relations Association (ARIR) evaluates listed companies. The final rating is then displayed on the Bucharest Stock Exchange website for each company. Starting with only three companies achieving a perfect score of ten in 2019, this number has now increased to 16. The methodology is modified annually by a committee comprising investors and analysts. This year, the focus has been on elements like quarterly conference calls, presentations, recordings, transcripts, translations and Excel. With numerous challenges arising each year, investors expect swift access to comparable and easily digestible data.

Daniela Maior (Serban)
President & Co-Founder
ROMANIAN IR ASSOCIATION

---

knowledge provide the profession with unique opportunities to grow its value proposition.

And when it comes to proof points, we have recent history on our side. Investor Relations' entire operating model was overturned when the world was overrun by a deadly virus in 2020. For professional communicators of all stripes and hues, Covid-19 meant, overnight, a profound shift to a new virtual role. But the crisis also further strengthened the reputation of investor relations, and its provable value, resulting in demonstrably higher share prices for firms that had the best IR functions.

In February 2023, research in the *Journal of Banking & Finance*[7], analyzing 1,000 publicly-traded companies in 16

The future of the profession depends on IROs truly demonstrating that they bring additional value—and to do that, we need to think laterally.

For example, if we take the IR unit of a bank, on top of the "usual suspects" (stock price, credit ratings), the institution would benefit from many interventions IR could directly influence: lower cost of debt and bank financing; lower cost of equity issuance; lower cost of insurance providers (both for traditional and ESG-related risks); investment-banking fees, should the IR unit pitch for an IPO candidate; lower cost of potential sanctions from poor financial communication; and so on. These sorts of true value-adds—proactive attention to what really matters to the company's commercial success—could be what makes the difference.

Piero Munari
**Co-Founder - Arwin&Partners
& Former Chair
ITALIAN INVESTOR RELATIONS SOCIETY**

---

[7] Neukirchen, Daniel, et al. "The value of (private) investor relations during the COVID-19 crisis." *Journal of Banking & Finance* 147 (2023): 106450.

countries, found that companies with strong IR outreach (based on their international IR rankings) experienced 5-8% higher stock returns during the Covid-19 pandemic than those with weaker IR ratings.

Furthermore, IR functions rated as "high-quality" not only attracted significantly more institutional investors during Covid-19, but also enjoyed higher credibility ratings with the firm's existing shareholder base. And it was the intimate, one-to-one, private IR outreach, such as continuing to organize direct meetings with senior management—rather than public communications—that were the main driver of all these uplifts. Indeed, interestingly, public IR did not appear to contribute to the outperformance of firms with better-quality IR at all.

Correlation between 'Satisfaction with IR' & 'Confidence in Management'

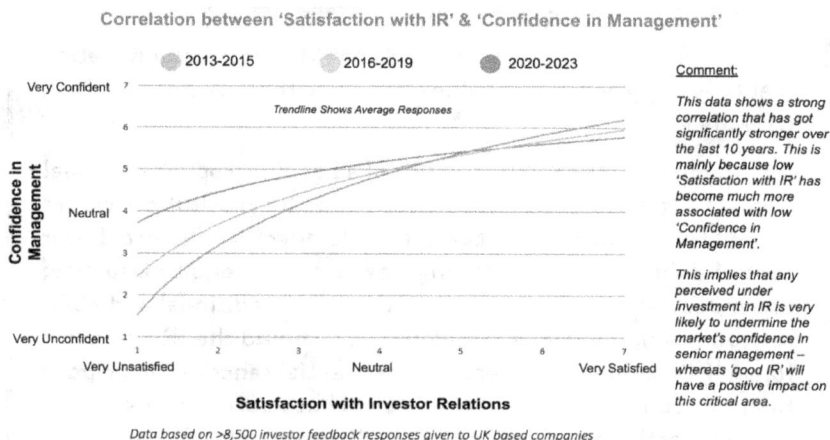

Data based on >8,500 investor feedback responses given to UK based companies

Quantifire analysis from a decade of shareholder surveys about the investor relations of UK companies is startling. It reveals a marked correlation — and an increasing one – between the quality of IR and investors' confidence levels in the company's management.

Especially in a world in which the public, more standardized parts of the IRO's role (e.g., reporting) are threatened with usurpation by AI and large language models, it's vital proof that the unique one-to-one capabilities of an accomplished IRO can have demonstrable impact on the company's bottom line.

Correlation between 'Satisfaction with IR' & 'Perception of Valuation'

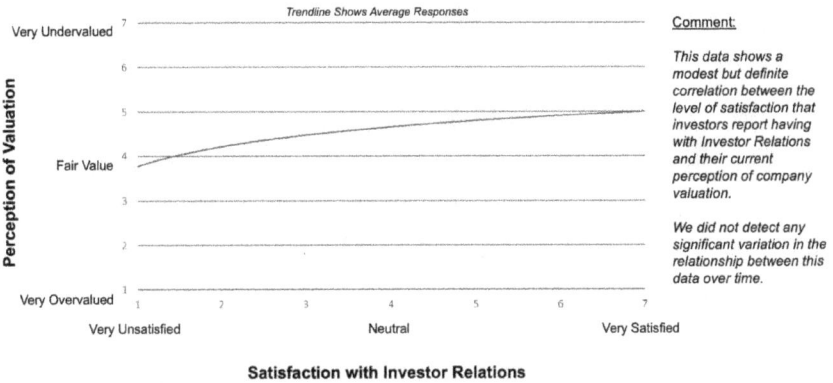

Comment:

This data shows a modest but definite correlation between the level of satisfaction that investors report having with Investor Relations and their current perception of company valuation.

We did not detect any significant variation in the relationship between this data over time.

Satisfaction with Investor Relations

Data based on >7,000 investor feedback responses given to UK based companies

Data from QuantiFire, analyzing 7,000 investor responses to questions on UK listed companies, found a clear correlation between investor perceptions about the quality of a company's IR and their perception of its valuation

An effective IR program should—in the future—be seen as an important component of any listed business's competitive advantage and for the contribution it makes to lowering its long-term cost of capital. I would like to see IR considered earlier in the process by pre-IPO companies. Equitory does a lot of work with international exchanges to educate on the value that IR brings to an IPO. Companies appoint a suite of advisers early in the process, including financial PR, yet too often overlook IR until just before, or just after listing, by which time it's too late for IR to add any value to the important first few trading days for a newly listed company.

Clara Melia
Founder and CEO
EQUITORY

What Investors Most Want from IROs

Top 10 most important areas

Receptiveness to Feedback

Business / Industry Knowledge

Detail

Proactivity

Responsiveness

Accessibility

Honesty & Transparency

Strategic Vision

Clarity

Expectations Management

Results based on an analysis of all investor feedback since 2013 where a comment was made in relation to the quality of service from an IR team.

1. **Responsive (31%):** Investors value teams that are responsive to their questions and requests for information.

2. **Honest and transparent (22%):** Open, honest, and transparent in all communications, providing candid answers and addressing concerns directly.

3. **Proactive (17%):** Proactive and communicative, providing regular and timely updates, information and access.

4. **Clear and Concise (16%):** Communications that are easy to understand, especially around key issues, avoiding jargon/technical terms whenever possible.

5. **Knowledgeable (15%):** Show a deep understanding of the company's business, industry dynamics, and market trends, providing additional valuable insights and analysis to investors.

6. **Accessible (13%):** Investors value regular opportunities to meet with senior management teams.

7. **Detailed & Granular (8%):** Information that allows them to better understand the current business activity, competitive dynamics, and market trends.

8. **Receptive (7%):** Willing to understand the opinions & perspectives of investors, and open to hearing their insights and concerns.

9. **Vision (5%):** Effectively communicate the company's long-term strategic vision and plans for growth.

10. **Effective Expectations Manager (5%):** Effectively manages market expectations and communicates well to market as a whole.

QuantiFire's analysis of more than 1000 investor survey responses over 2013-2023: What investors value most from IROs

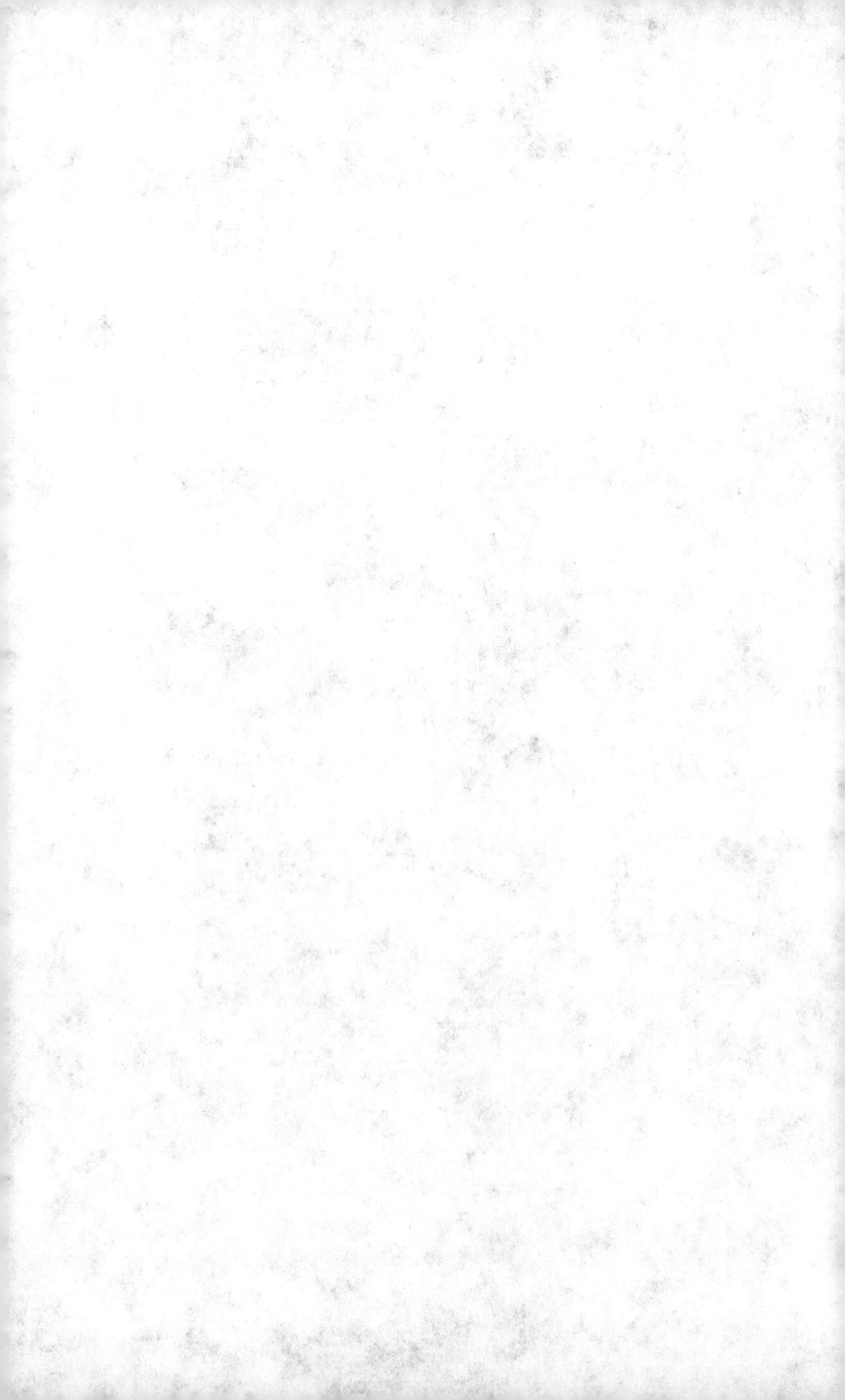

6. CONCLUSIONS

Stand out or stand aside—the future is ours!

STAND OUT OR STAND ASIDE

O ur industry has come a long way—that is clearly evidenced by the findings of this book, which have been based not just on 200 in-depth interviews but the wider input of several hundred IROs and capital-markets professionals as well as feedback from more than 2,000 interviews with senior IROs over the past 20 years.

The clear indications are that IR will only continue to grow and strengthen its reputation at C-Suite level, as well as with the full range of market stakeholders. And by coming together to celebrate how far we have come—and to pinpoint where and how much more we can do—has been tantalizing, because it has revealed that the growth and development of our industry is no longer just an idle, hopeful ambition. Our biggest takeaway at Broome Yasar has been that our industry, and those within it, now have the world at their feet—if they can force themselves to see it shrouded by their daily to-do lists!

Salaries and career trajectories have increased significantly— this is reflected through the data we have been privy to from thousands of interviews over the last two decades. It's clear that compensation has accelerated in recent years, due entirely to the fact that both reputation and IR is now a board level agenda topic coupled with the fact that there has been a tsunami of ambitious, financially bolted and incredibly sophisticated new entrants into IR. This book, I hasten to add, is not a salary survey and I believe that anyone who thinks they know what the average comp is for an IRO in your region is either telling a lie or has misjudged the data— how can there be an average comp when salaries for the same role, same market capitalization and same sector can vary in excess of, in some case, more than $100k. There is therefore no average!

> I believe it's a time of great hope. The IR function is becoming more and more valued. And, given the broader career experiences and higher education levels within the profession (CFA, IRC, CPA, etc.), IROs now have greater opportunities to transition into other management roles like operations, strategy or CFO.
>
> *Ashish Kohli*
> **VP Investor Relations**
> **GENERAL MOTORS**

IROS MOVING ON TO SENIOR EXECUTIVE ROLES

In recent years, many of the IR leaders we work with at Broome Yasar have successfully transitioned into senior business leadership roles—not just heads of strategy or development, but they have also broadened their responsibilities to take on the whole corporate affairs remit. Some have become CFOs, even CEOs and with many now being put onto listed boards as independent/non-executive directors. Let me repeat that as it's an extraordinary development —some have become CEOs, CFOs and Independent/Non-Executive Directors. Truly, our industry has come a very long way in a few, short years.

There are still several leading figures in the round who do not believe this; who have not adjusted to the strong, powerful and influential industry we are today. This book goes some way to highlighting that strength—and, indeed, to proving that (contrary to the beliefs of the cynics) ours is indeed an *industry*.

THE PRESSURES ON SENIOR MANAGEMENT AND WHAT OUR INDUSTRY NEEDS TO DO TO PROTECT THEM

Changing financial and regulatory dynamics in recent years have evidently put an extraordinary amount of pressure on senior management, straining relationships with the markets and altering how companies put together a coherent and disciplined IR program. It's these pressures that have resulted in not just the role of IR and its programs being taken more seriously by the Board, but by the markets too.

It means that we are at a moment of reckoning, and IROs—and CEOs and CFOs—need to be aware of the key vectors shaping investor relations right now, if they want to effectively navigate this evolving business landscape over the coming years. Much of that future is already upon us, and the spoils of victory will go to those who choose the correct course to overcome its many challenges.

KEY CHALLENGES FACING GLOBAL IR

It has been clear throughout this book that the landscape of global investor relations is poised for significant transformation, driven by a dynamic interplay of technological advancements, regulatory changes, and evolving stakeholder expectations. Among these, we can also see several specific challenges facing IR:

> **Digital disruption:**
> The rise of digital platforms and the acceleration of technological innovations have altered the way information is disseminated and consumed. IR

professionals must adapt to the digital era, leveraging data analytics and AI for more accurate insights into investor behavior.

> **Regulatory complexity:**
Increasing regulatory requirements demand a heightened focus on compliance. Navigating the complex regulatory landscape across different jurisdictions poses a challenge, necessitating a proactive approach.

> **Evolving stakeholder expectations:**
Stakeholders, including institutional investors and retail shareholders, now expect more transparency and engagement. IR professionals must find innovative ways to communicate company strategies and performance to meet diverse stakeholder expectations.

> **Environmental, Social, and Governance (ESG) integration:**
ESG considerations are now integral to investment decisions. Any IR function that hasn't done so already, therefore, must evolve to incorporate robust ESG reporting, demonstrating a commitment to sustainable and responsible business practices.

> **Global economic uncertainty:**
Economic volatility and geopolitical uncertainties impact investor confidence. IR professionals must develop strategies to navigate through unpredictable economic conditions, providing clarity and assurance to investors.

You don't need to be an IT geek to work in IR, but you need to understand how these technologies work, how AI will affect your output or bring in tools that make your life easier. And that is changing constantly. ChatGPT is different now to how it was two months ago, and it will be different again next year. So you need to stay on top of all these digital changes.

Then what are the right digital channels? Do you need to talk to influencers? How could that affect your rating? How do you speak to Gen Z? They don't read the newspapers you're traditionally accustomed to talking to. They've got Instagram and TikTok, so how do you feed those channels? When I was starting in IR, it was all about the elevator pitch: Explain what you're doing in two minutes. Now you have to explain what you're doing in six seconds.

Kay Bommer
Managing Director
GERMAN IR SOCIETY (DIRK)

The future challenges for IR

By Cas Sydorowitz, Global CEO, GEORGESON

There are several factors changing the landscape for IROs globally.

> **Growth in passive investors,** where there is no portfolio manager making buy or sell decisions, your inclusion in an index makes you a guaranteed holding of that product with no one to meet or talk to. They will own your stock through good and bad times but there is nothing you as an IRO can do to impact their ownership.

> **Growth in retail investors,** allowing them to trade commission-free and purchase partial shares, which make stocks more accessible to a new audience of retail investors—who, by way of research, spend more time on Instagram and TikTok than on their own fundamental analysis, who trade on their phones and are less interested in the ongoing news flow around the company and are more focused on share price performance. These investors are being asked by their brokers (and/or the platforms) to set up voting policies and rules that will allow them to vote on their shares based on blanket policies applied to their whole portfolio.

> **A shrinking pool of asset managers,** who continue to consolidate and merge to address rising costs of legal and compliance, and reporting requirements. This yields fewer names to attract to the equity story in a crowded space of public companies. It is creating an environment where companies are staying private longer and accessing alternate funding pools to provide liquidity

and operating capital. Private markets are proving more liquid allowing companies to consider alternative options to public markets.

Whether it's a public company or a private company, what investors want to know from the companies they invest in—the scope of the key financial, environmental and human-capital risks—will increase, and IROs will need to be able to identify and articulate what those risks are and how they impact the company and its policies.

CATALYSTS FOR THE FUTURE OF GLOBAL IR

How, then, should the function respond? Feedback from our interviews and analysis of hundreds of candidate interviews tells us that the future of IR lies in:

> Technology integration
> Embracing advanced technologies such as AI and Blockchain can enhance data accuracy, automate routine tasks, and provide deeper insights into investor behavior, ultimately improving decision-making processes.

> Data-driven decision making
> Leveraging big data analytics enables IR professionals to gain actionable insights, helping us craft more targeted and effective communication strategies. Data-driven decision-making is key to anticipating investor needs and concerns.

Investors today demand far deeper underlying knowledge from IROs on ESG and the long-term sustainability strategy. For similar reasons, they also now expect the IRO to be an expert in not just the business but the industry sector, to display a full picture of the evolving regulatory environment and to anticipate future trends.

Perhaps as a result, we also see investors prizing long-term IR teams. Team turnover is very much disliked: Investors expect IROs to be fully on top of these questions, and that can't happen when knowledge keeps leaving the team. So stability is now a greater priority than ever before, as is the need for IROs to work on a number of assignments related to ratings (e.g., ESG, Credit). And a very close cooperation and coordination needs to be created between the IR and ESG unit.

Piero Munari
Co-Founder - Arwin&Partners
& Former Chair
ITALIAN INVESTOR RELATIONS SOCIETY

> Enhanced stakeholder engagement:
  Digital channels, webinars, and virtual meetings have
  become a given since the pandemic and they are here
  to stay—that is now a fact. IROs need to focus on the
  positives from this (i.e., virtual meetings help facilitate
  more frequent and interactive communication with
  stakeholders) while also taking it to the next level,
  developing customized and personalized approaches to
  build stronger relationships through these channels.

> **Integrated ESG reporting**
  Embedding ESG metrics into financial reporting
  demonstrates a commitment to sustainability, and have
  fast become a standard, expected part of the IR portfolio.
  Any top-tier IR function today should be collaborating
  closely with sustainability teams to provide comprehensive
  information that aligns with evolving ESG standards.

IR is at an exciting crossroads. Like all players in capital markets, the decline in the number of listed companies is a headwind—fewer companies means fewer roles. The growth of the ever-acquisitive private equity machine significantly shifts the relationship between Board and shareholders: The comms is much simpler when those shareholders control the Board.

But for those companies that stay in the quoted arena, new opportunities abound. Fewer quoted peers means it should be easier to stand out and this is where the best IROs will excel. The role is more complex than ever and encompasses a much wider remit. As a result, it is growing in importance and so budgets to support the function must also grow.

Fraser Thorne
Chief Executive
EDISON GROUP

> **Agile regulatory compliance**
> Developing agile compliance frameworks allows IR
> professionals to stay ahead of regulatory changes.
> Continuous monitoring, adapting internal processes, and
> utilizing technology for compliance management are
> crucial in this regard.

> **Global collaboration and cultural sensitivity**
> As businesses operate in a globalized environment, IR must
> be sensitive to cultural nuances and collaborate across
> diverse markets. Understanding regional expectations
> and tailoring communication strategies accordingly
> fosters trust.

It's clear that the future direction of the global IR profession
hinges on its ability to navigate challenges, embrace
technological advancements, and adapt to evolving stakeholder
expectations. By integrating these core themes into their
practices, IR professionals can not only overcome obstacles but
also elevate the industry to unprecedented levels of effectiveness
and transparency.

In terms of the day-to-day role, I think IROs will increasingly
need to employ systems or people focused on management and
AI-driven analysis of digital data. They will need to be able to
think about automation of processes, on the one hand, and be
more strategic on the other. In a world where there is likely to be
demand for more social media and online content, the line could
become more blurred as to who "owns" the corporate, strategic
messaging and what it is.

Karen Keyes
Head of Investor Relations
CANADIAN TIRE CORPORATION

By keeping a watchful eye on these trends and proactively adjusting their IR strategies, CEOs and CFOs, too, can ensure that their organizations are well-positioned to navigate the evolving investor relations landscape over the next decade.

TAKING A STEP UP TO "NEXT LEVEL" IR

We all need to consider adopting innovative strategies and practices to continue not only to strengthen our reputation but also to increase share of voice at the C-Suite—and for us to build a truly global profession, with a standard operating model and universally agreed competencies. In other words, a recognized industry—not just a set of individual jobs.

How do we raise the whole profession? Everyone needs to play a part. Leading IROs must use their unique power to establish IR as a recognized profession—to stay here and build something, not just move on to the next role. IR associations should raise our profile by integrating C-Suite personnel into some of their keynote events, and encourage them to 'spread the word' among their networks. Search firms aware of IR talent languishing in organizations that don't get the value of the role could support the flow of talent where it can flourish better. And associations should also ensure that IR professionals are able to continuously develop their skills outside of on-the-job training.

Philip Ludwig
Vice-Chair
BELGIAN IR ASSOCIATION &
Investor Relations Director
MELEXIS

> **Crisis preparedness and communication plans**
>
> Develop comprehensive crisis communication plans to address unforeseen events promptly and transparently. Preparedness and proactive communication during crises can help maintain investor trust and mitigate potential reputational damage—ultimately to be part of that wave whereby senior IROs are now taking over the corporate communications narrative and function in a significant number of organizations. Put bluntly, should ownership of the core company narrative be controlled by IR? A number of Boards think it should!

> **Embrace technology and data analytics**
>
> Leverage advanced technologies, including artificial intelligence and data analytics, to gain deeper insights into investor behavior. Implement tools that enable real-time monitoring, predictive analytics, and customized reporting to enhance decision-making processes.

> **Digitalize communication channels**
>
> Embrace digital communication channels, such as social media, webcasts, and virtual meetings, to reach a broader audience. Develop interactive and engaging content to enhance communication with both institutional and retail investors, fostering a sense of transparency and accessibility.

> **Prioritize ESG Reporting**
>
> Integrate ESG considerations into reporting practices. Develop robust ESG metrics and disclosure frameworks to provide investors with comprehensive information about the company's sustainability efforts, fostering trust and attracting socially conscious investors.

> **Enhance transparency and accessibility**
> Prioritize transparency by providing clear and easily accessible information about the company's financial performance, strategies, and risks. Utilize technology to streamline reporting processes and make relevant information readily available to investors.

> **Proactive regulatory compliance**
> Stay ahead of evolving regulatory requirements globally. Develop proactive compliance strategies, keeping in mind the potential impact of regulatory changes on investor relations practices. Establish strong relationships with regulatory bodies to ensure a collaborative and informed approach.

> **Investor education programs**
> Develop educational programs for investors to enhance their understanding of the company's industry, market

---

As we look to the future of Investor Relations, we shouldn't be fooled by the promises surrounding ESG and artificial intelligence. True, they are instruments of change, but the future of IR lies on the same axis as always: in a constant reinvention, where regulatory changes and technology innovation are enabling forces, rather than inhibitors. It "takes two to tango" for this constant reinvention to succeed: A CEO with an ROI mindset (where IR is part of the capital allocation framework) and a steadfast commitment to maintaining the fundamentals of IR for what they are: fundamental. It is all about being truthful, accurate, complete, objective, consistent, timely and understandable. That will not change.

Anne Guimard
Founder & President
FINEO INVESTOR RELATIONS ADVISORS

---

dynamics, and long-term strategies. This can lead to more informed investment decisions and foster a positive perception of the company.

> **Cultural competence for global operations**
> Build cultural competence within the IR team to navigate diverse markets successfully. Tailor communication strategies to suit different cultural expectations, fostering stronger relationships with a global investor base.

> **Innovative stakeholder engagement**
> Implement innovative strategies for stakeholder engagement. Consider virtual events, online forums, and interactive platforms to enhance communication with investors. Solicit feedback and address concerns promptly to demonstrate a commitment to shareholder value.

> **Long-term value communication**
> Shift the focus from short-term gains to long-term value creation. Communicate the company's strategies

---

Ultimately, the future of IR depends upon the talent pool that it draws upon. The success of IR over the last ten years has been predicated on the incredibly diverse range of talented professionals that have come in and changed and expanded the role.

This, I think, has now become a flywheel. Because the IR remit has become broad, challenging and rewarding, it has become a more attractive team to aspire to join than it once was. The people we are now attracting and developing are showing significantly greater potential than I did when I started ten years ago.

Matthew Johnson
Group Communications Director,
IR & CEO Office,
VODAFONE

---

for sustainable growth and emphasize investments in innovation, employee well-being, and environmental responsibility to attract investors with a long-term perspective.

> **Continuous professional development**
Invest in the continuous professional development of IR professionals. Equip the team with the latest skills, knowledge, and industry best practices to stay ahead of trends and navigate evolving challenges effectively.

> **Collaboration with other departments**
Foster collaboration between IR and other departments, such as marketing, sustainability, and legal teams. Cross-functional collaboration ensures a holistic approach to communication and reporting, aligning with overall corporate goals.

By adopting these strategies, IR professionals can contribute to the growth and resilience of the industry, enhancing its reputation as an essential component of corporate success and transparent communication with the investment community.

The future? Investors, markets and regulations are all constantly evolving, so the IR profession will have to keep pushing itself to raise its level constantly if it is to thrive—not just thinking about how to use IR leadership as a stepping stone to becoming CFO or head of strategy, but how to ensure that senior IR professionals are themselves increasingly considered management.

Javier Rodriguez-Vega
Managing Director
SPANISH ASSOCIATION FOR IR (AERI)

STRENGTHENING OUR INDUSTRY'S VOICE

And what do we all need to do as IR professionals to bolster the industry and continue to strengthen its reputation over the next ten years?

> **Raise your profile**
> IROs who feel undervalued in their organizations need to use all the tools in IR's unique armory—evidenced by the many examples from practitioners littered throughout this book—to reshape their role internally and look for better ways to deliver value. Become a member of your local IR society and benchmark with your peers. Use research data (such as that provided by QuantiFire in this report) to make the case internally for management leveraging more value from IR. Build your personal brand—get credentialled in your regional association's accreditation and certification programs.

> **Build the profession—not just yourself**
> But especially top-tier IROs perhaps have an even more crucial role here. Because those who have already achieved leadership status for the function—and who have persuasive intent and the desire to be part of a rising discipline—have

---

IR's future will be determined by its own effectiveness and through trailblazers who show others how it can be done. The exact value to the C-suite of an effective IR function is different for different CEOs and CFOs and different companies. I do think that the number of IROs on executive management teams will be a determining factor in its future success.

Debbie Millar
Chair
IR SOCIETY OF SOUTH AFRICA

---

a unique opportunity to change the entire global profession. Too often, these senior talents use the IRO role as a stepping stone to other leadership positions. Imagine if, instead, they utilized their talents to stay in IR and make it the most attractive place to be in the leadership hierarchy.

> **Promote globalism**
  Perhaps more than any other group, these high flyers have the opportunity to make IR a recognized global profession. And that is what we need to be: We must come together as a global industry and create a sense of a global profession. Here, country associations have a major role to play. We need interconnectedness—collaboration on research; unification of credentialling programs to create international equivalence; and more effort to build collaborative, global events between them.

The main issue for IR as an industry is not the talent base or skills shortages but a wider lack of knowledge about our profession. We need more publicity about what IR is and can do.

But we will get there: Each new crisis—inflation, recession, deglobalization, trade wars—becomes an opportunity for IR to make a difference by educating leaders about emerging risks, and externally by affecting investment decisions in a changing world. Each leaves a mark, creating more recognition of the value IR can bring. Each time IR creates a clear equity story people buy into, a corporate strategy has been built and explained. And the best IR teams are excellent at increasing trust in the company: That is our profession's key currency and will remain paramount in the next years and decades.

So I see IR gradually continuing to increase in importance, albeit slowly. But the key to that happening at an individual level is to get yourself seen, heard and recognized.

Constantin Fest
SVP/Head of IR
GSK

EXCEED YOUR BOUNDARIES

This is the first time we have come together to not just showcase the revolution going on within the IR industry internationally, but to outline what we all need to do—every single one of us—to strengthen its reputation, visibility and credibility.

As the leading IR executive recruiter, global partners Broome Yasar and PLBsearch wanted to highlight—to our ever-changing industry, and to the new entrants now surging into it—where we have come from as a profession, where we now sit and, more importantly, where we are all heading. We recognized that we were living through a historic inflection point in IR, but what we lacked was a true blueprint for our future direction and destiny. It became our mission to go out and speak to the leading lights in our profession to help set that course.

Through this research, it is clear that we are incredibly well-positioned now to capitalize on a unique moment. For 75 years, our function has been in a constant process of re-invention, going through periods of evolution punctuated by sudden moments of radical revolution. We have proven each time that we are adaptable to changing circumstances, able to flex to the needs of new eras, and to find new ways to deliver value to ensure we always stay relevant, whatever the circumstances. That has been the calling card of our profession from its very beginnings.

Never has that capability been more important than now. For, without question, the most recent of these moments of change has been a revolutionary one—a dramatic heightening of the status and authority of the profession, as a result of vastly increased expectations at the highest levels of major organizations. Senior management now realizes how dependent their careers are on their ability to communicate with their financial stakeholders, and that they need a reliable proxy sitting at their right hand— credible, smart, informed and with the business acumen to make the right judgement calls when required.

Gone are the days of IR being seen as a box-ticking exercise, or of IROs being little more than a glorified bag carrier for the CEO. We now sit at the top table—in the C-Suite when key decisions are being made. By laying that out clearly in this book, our hope is that you will take confidence from it—and take on the mantle of driving the industry even further forward.

Many IROs we speak to are now broadening their authority, taking ownership of the corporate affairs mantle in response to this generational shift, recognizing that the remits of IR and corporate affairs are beginning to converge at executive level— with both functions expected to shoulder the responsibility for air-traffic-controlling the company's reputation; both needing to own and steer their company narrative. Many

---

As AI and other technologies develop further, and with the rise of activist investors, IR will increasingly have to become about "more than numbers." I think IR will focus more on personal elements of communication and will involve higher level work in this regard— communications strategies, ESG issues, sustainability reporting and more. My forecast? The developing professionalization of IR within companies, coupled with the needs of the capital markets and investors, will eventually lead to the IRO operating at the same level, and being considered as mandatory, as the CFO role.

Iris Golani
Founder & Director
ISRAELI IR FORUM (IIRF)
ISRAELI ASSOCIATION OF PUBLICLY
TRADED COMPANIES

---

other IROs are now moving on to broader leadership roles. More importantly, we are now seeing them take up CFO and CEO positions in some of the world's largest organizations (as covered in our previous study, *From IR to Business Leadership*).

All of that tells us something else, from a talent perspective. To fulfill that new, authoritative role, we are witnessing a change in the talent profile—the arrival of a more powerful, more astute and more sophisticated IRO. Many are now armed with CFAs, ACAs and MBAs. They bring sophistication and credibility. They bring different backgrounds (often sectoral experience, rather than communications or financial expertise). More than that, they bring ambition. One thing we are quick to ignore is what an attractive profession the world of IR has become.

I think the function has never been more integrated with management and the business. It has never been more challenging to work in IR and that is also recognized by management. It requires more in-depth knowledge about the business, including insights outside financial numbers and business value drivers. The changes to the sophistication in the past five to ten years have been material as a result—IR today needs a far broader and more in-depth knowledge of the company and has a far broader set of responsibilities: ESG regulation, ESG frameworks, ESG raters, and so on, as well as the fact that IR also supports conversations with debt markets, insurance markets and investor organizations around non-financial developments. People are starting to stay in IR teams longer as a result because it's diverse and interesting work, and that reflects something profound: It's truly a great time to work in this profession.

Andreas Bork
Vice-President, IR & ESG
SHELL

All of this puts IR in an incredibly strong position as it faces the future. And it needs that strength, because looming on the horizon are many great uncertainties due to the changing investor landscape, the arrival of AI, the rise of activist shareholders, the decline in listed companies, and much more. We hope this book goes some way to demonstrating what an amazing platform IR now has globally to meet these challenges, and to build towards future success.

Those with direct experience as investor relations professionals know there is no other corporate role quite like IR. Positioned at the nexus of internal and external communications, IR professionals have a unique opportunity to positively influence corporate strategy and transparency for the benefit of their companies and, ultimately, their stakeholders.

Matt Brusch
President and CEO
NIRI: The Association for Investor Relations

I believe that IR as a profession, over the next ten to 20 years, will continue to evolve in a positive way. You'll see IROs being considered equivalent to CFOs (or approaching equivalence). You'll see IROs being elevated to CFO roles more often and having greater involvement and engagement with Boards. Additionally, you'll continue to see a greater use of technology to analyze, distribute and report information to constituents (although investors will still need to "see the whites of your eyes" and personal connection will not go away). Personal and corporate reputation will remain of paramount importance in IR.

Laura Kiernan
Senior Vice President
RIVEL, INC

The more we come together and shout about how great we are and bang that drum as hard as possible, the more people will listen. It's an easy equation and we're confident that our industry will continue to strengthen and, ultimately, that we will see many more examples of former IROs becoming the next major business titans.

As we regularly say to all our senior candidates, clients and wider network, our careers are only limited by our own ambition. That can now be easily said about our industry. *Our industry is now only limited by its own ambition.* Onwards and upwards!

Oskar Yasar
Managing Partner
Broome Yasar Partnership

7. ABOUT THIS RESEARCH

RESEARCH METHODOLOGY AND INTERVIEWEES

Through 2023 and 2024, we interviewed more than 200 leading IROs and the heads of IR associations in 17 different countries or regions, from the US to Hong Kong, from Europe and the Middle East to Australia along with data from more than 2,000 confidential interviews with some of the leading IROs globally.

Australia
Ian Matheson
CEO
AUSTRALASIAN INVESTOR RELATIONS ASSOCIATION

Belgium
Philip Ludwig
Vice-Chair
BELGIAN IR ASSOCIATION

Canada
Nathalie Megann
President and Chief Executive Officer
CANADIAN IR INSTITUTE (CIRI)

Germany
Kay Bommer
Managing Director
GERMAN INVESTOR RELATIONS SOCIETY (DIRK)

Hong Kong
Eva Chan
Chair
HONG KONG IR ASSOCIATION

Israel
Iris Golani
Founder & Director
ISRAELI INVESTOR RELATIONS FORUM (IIRF)
ISRAELI ASSOCIATION OF PUBLICLY TRADED COMPANIES

Italy
Piero Munari
Co-Founder - Arwin&Partners
& Former Chair
ITALIAN INVESTOR RELATIONS SOCIETY

Mexico
Maximilian Zimmermann Canovas
Investor Relations and Sustainability Director
GRUPO HOTELERO SANTA FE
President and Co-founder
MEXICAN INSTITUTE FOR INVESTOR RELATIONS (INARI)

Middle East
Paolo Casamassima & John Gollifer (Current and former)
Chief Executive Officer
MEIRA (THE MIDDLE EAST IR ASSOCIATION)

The Netherlands
Andreas Bork
Vice-President, IR & ESG
SHELL
Former Chair of the Board
THE NETHERLANDS ASSOCIATION FOR IR (NEVIR)

Romania
Daniela Maior (Serban)
President & Co-Founder
Romanian Investor Relations Association

South Africa
Debbie Millar
Chair
IR SOCIETY OF SOUTH AFRICA

Spain
Javier Rodriguez-Vega
Managing Director
SPANISH ASSOCIATION FOR INVESTOR RELATIONS (AERI)

Switzerland
Lorna Davie
President
IR CLUB SWITZERLAND
& Former Director, Investor Relations
CREDIT SUISSE/UBS

Turkey
Başak Öge
Chair
TURKISH IR SOCIETY
& Corporate Governance & Compliance Coordinator
TÜRKİYE ŞİŞE VE CAM FABRİKALARI A.Ş

UK
Laura Hayter
CEO
THE INVESTOR RELATIONS SOCIETY, UK

USA
Matt Brusch
President and CEO
NIRI: The Association for Investor Relations

RESEARCH
PARTNERS &
BIBLIOGRAPHY

We are also grateful to select partner organizations and associations for the insights, analytics, data contributions, permission to reproduce existing proprietary research, and other contributions to this book. Notably:

- *IR IMPACT*

  Insights, intelligence and influence for real IR impact

  IR Impact is the global leader in investor relations intelligence, providing IR professionals with the insights, data and connections they need to navigate the evolving capital markets. For more than 35 years, it has been the trusted voice of the IR community, delivering expert content, research and events that drive smarter decision-making. Its platform helps IROs elevate the profession, make a greater impact and stay ahead in a rapidly changing financial landscape.

  https://www.ir-impact.com/

- *EXTEL:*

  Extel surveys of the buy side, sell side and C-Suite and IR teams have set the standard in using accountability and transparency to drive performance improvement. It measures what really matters and empowers customers to make smarter decisions.

  https://www.extelinsights.com/

- ### *NIRI: THE ASSOCIATION FOR INVESTOR RELATIONS*

The oldest and biggest national IR association, US-based NIRI was established in 1969 and today has more than 3,300 members representing over 1,600 publicly held companies and $9 trillion in stock market capitalization.

www.niri.org

In this report, we gratefully reproduce NIRI's data with permission from:

The Disruption Opportunity: A report of the NIRI Think Tank on the future of investor relations (2019)

- ### *QUANTIFIRE*

UK-based QuantiFire analyzes the needs and interests of investor communities, as data, at scale. QuantiFire has analyzed responses to more than 500,000 questions submitted by investors at over 5,000 institutions, including almost every significant investment institution globally.

www.quantifire.co.uk

Throughout this report, with gratitude, we reproduce QuantiFire's data from:

IR Society Members Feedback (annual surveys, 2013-2023)

- ### *STORYLINE COMMUNICATIONS*

Storyline Communications has been researching the global corporate affairs and investor relations industries for 25 years, publishing thousands of case studies of best practice and regular, award-winning research into ongoing developments in corporate communications. We are grateful to them for their research, analysis and copywriting services for this report.

www.storyline-communications.com

INTRODUCING BROOME YASAR PARTNERSHIP

W e are regarded as the global leader in investor relations and corporate affairs executive recruitment along with our position as the home of thought leadership on our ever-evolving industries.

We founded Broome Yasar Partnership in 2013, a unique executive search firm centered not just on curating close relationships with our clients and all the highest quality professionals in corporate affairs and investor relations, but on working with them continuously over years to improve their capabilities through assessment, skills training, coaching, and career focused thought leadership like this book.

It has resulted in helping to appoint more than 500 senior level corporate affairs and investor relations leadership roles, guaranteeing our clients a constantly high level of quality because the development work we do with the best people in the field gives us insight into their true, underlying capabilities. Meanwhile, our research work including this book gives us a direct line into the strategic and commercial ebb and flow of the profession as a whole.

And it's why, from our foundation, we have committed to driving up the standards of the profession through our own daily work—by conducting ground-breaking primary research, publishing leadership papers for industry journals, speaking at events, running bespoke benchmarking projects for multinationals, and being lead members of our core industries' professional associations.

By building an international partnership of interconnected, boutique, executive search consultancies in key markets including PLBsearch in the US and Andrews Partnership in Asia—we could keep things at the right scale, with each of us curating personal relationships with the best local senior talent, and still having time to do the day job: Getting the best people into the best roles. The reputation for high quality we have built since then speaks for itself.

It is why our name has become our brand and why it's the kitemark of quality in the ever-evolving corporate affairs and investor relations professions.

www.broomeyasar.com